Robert F. Kennedy:
The Brother Within

Robert F. Kennedy:
The Brother Within

by Robert E. Thompson
and Hortense Myers

The Macmillan Company, New York

CONTENTS

FOREWORD: The biography of a living man is pieced together from such a multitude of sources that all cannot be acknowledged by the authors.

A bit of recollection over cocktails may work itself into several paragraphs. A few remarks dropped in casual conversation may develop into several pages. A single interview may prove the nucleus for an entire chapter. Volumes of newspaper and magazine articles and books must be devoured. Some provide a wealth of material. Others prove of little use.

It is impossible for the authors to list all individuals and publications that have proved of assistance in the writing of this book. But we are deeply indebted to all who have taken time—some from the world's busiest schedules—to discuss the subject of this biography with us.

Our particular gratitude to President John F. Kennedy, Attorney General Robert F. Kennedy, Mrs. Robert F. Kennedy, Former Ambassador Joseph P. Kennedy and Mrs. Joseph P. Kennedy.

Our special thanks also to: Hugh Sidey of Time *Magazine; those members of the United States Senate who were willing to express their honest and critical view of Robert Kennedy—Barry Goldwater of Arizona; Karl Mundt of South Dakota, and Homer Capehart of Indiana; Associate Justice Byron White; Kenneth O'Donnell; John Siegenthaler, now editor of the Nashville* Tennessean; *Edwin O. Guthman; David Powers; Angela Novello; Ruth Watt; Clinton Green; Burt Myers of* USA I; *Paul Healy of the New York* News; *Clarence Mitchell of the NAACP; K. LeMoyne Billings; Alvin Spivak of United Press International, and others who graciously offered assistance.*

Among book references, we wish to acknowledge five that proved invaluable: Robert Kennedy's "The Enemy Within," Joe McCarthy's "The Remarkable Kennedys," James MacGregor Burns' "John F. Kennedy, A Political Profile," Hugh Sidey's chapter in "The Kennedy Circle," and Richard Rovere's "Senator Joe McCarthy."

INTRODUCTION: My ties with Robert F. Kennedy have been so close that my appraisal of him and my reaction to what others say about him cannot be objective and dispassionate. I knew him long before he knew me, for my association with his father started with Franklin Roosevelt's first term when Robert Kennedy was a boy. Joseph P. Kennedy was, indeed, responsible for my coming to Washington, D.C. From the early 1930s I was a frequent visitor in the Kennedy home and saw Robert Kennedy grow to manhood.

It was, however, when he entered law school at Charlottesville that I came to know Robert Kennedy as a mature person. In the years since then I have seen him grow in stature as he gained experience in practical affairs both in and out of government. In 1955 we traveled Soviet Russia together and I saw how that trip, like earlier and subsequent ones, was helping him to become one of the most knowledgeable persons we have in world affairs. I knew then that one day he and his wife, Ethel (who joined us in Moscow), would be able to show even faraway illiterate villagers the warm heart and the bright conscience of America. Their reputation as our best Ambassadors-at-large is now firmly established.

Robert Kennedy pondered long before he told the President he would serve as Attorney General. He and I talked at length about it. I told him there was no doubt that he was qualified and would serve with distinction, that the voices of those who would criticize the appointment would be drowned out by his achievements. The question for him and Ethel, I ventured to say, was whether that office at that time fitted the pattern of the professional career he had for himself. It was obvious that Robert Kennedy's interests were and are far wider than law practice. In 1961 his alternatives, as I saw them, were either a college presidency or a high post in the State Department where his energy and genius could keep us from the dangerous drift that results when the clash of opposing views is so strong and bewildering that no *consensus* is reached.

In accepting the Cabinet post in the Department of Justice, Robert Kennedy undertook administrative work which he did not relish. Yet it was quickly evident that his varied talents were well suited to that task.

Apart from this particular episode, this book appears to give an accurate factual account of this young man's life to date. The major defects are in those passages that try to catalog him. Robert Kennedy has a unique capacity for growth. He thrives under responsibility and increases in stature with each job. I do not know what his long range ambitions may be; and while some would like to see him narrow them to a single target, he is too wise to do so. Public service, however, is his career. His present office derives, of course, from his brother, the President. But he stands on his own and will arrive on his own at whatever high destination manifest destiny has reserved for him.

WILLIAM O. DOUGLAS

July 9, 1962

*   *   *   *   *   *   *

When Robert F. Kennedy wrote *"The Enemy Within"* he dedicated it to his wife Ethel with the explanation that her *"love through this long period made the difficult easy, the impossible possible."*

On Christmas, 1960, less than two months after John F. Kennedy had been elected President of the United States with the indispensible assistance of his brother, the President-elect and his wife, Jacqueline, presented Robert F. Kennedy with a copy of *"The Enemy Within"* that had been especially bound in red leather in London.

On the first page of the book, Jacqueline wrote: *"To Bobby—who made the impossible possible and changed all our lives. With love, Jackie."*

Below his wife's inscription, the President-elect, utilizing a lighter approach and less legible script, wrote: *"For Bobby—The Brother Within—who made the easy difficult. Jack, Christmas 1960."*

Chapter One
Decision

THE SECOND WEEK OF NOVEMBER, 1960, WAS THE TIME of the disturbance for residents of the picturesque village of Hyannis, Massachusetts, where shops and tourist homes stood idle after a bustling summer, and adjoining Hyannisport, where mansions of the rich had been shuttered for the winter.

Local folk in this New England resort community, where tradition dictates a Republican vote on election day and a lethargic pace from Labor Day to Memorial Day, were dismayed that the presence of a lone Democrat in their midst had shattered their tranquillity.

Hundreds of newspaper reporters, hordes of police and secret service agents, truckloads of television and newsreel equipment, and carloads of spectators burst upon the village like a blitzkrieg.

Focal point of the disturbance was a fenced-in oceanfront compound where stood three sprawling white frame houses. The largest of the dwellings, with great windows looking out upon sulking, rainswept Nantucket Sound, was the property of seventy-two-year-old Joseph Patrick Kennedy. Beside it stood the home of Robert Francis Kennedy, and slightly behind it, the home of John Fitzgerald Kennedy.

Although the raw late autumn wind carried alternating showers across the Sound on November 9, 1960, the weather could not work its despair upon the occupants of the houses within the compound. A glow of restrained good spirit filled the three homes because it appeared that John Kennedy had won a victory against two of the most awesome obstacles in American politics—religious prejudice and the mistrust of youth.

The glow was restrained for two reasons. First, Kennedy self-discipline does not permit an effusion of tears or a profusion of sentiment even at the most triumphant moments. Secondly, the victory was an exceedingly wobbly one.

Sometime shortly after midnight of November 8, Senator Kennedy, forty-three years old and the eldest of seven living children of Joseph P. Kennedy and his wife, Rose, was reported to have captured the 269 electoral votes needed to make him the thirty-fifth President of the United States.

The nation's press, radio and television and even his opponent, Vice President Richard M. Nixon, had declared Kennedy the victor. But as the hours went by, the margin of victory kept dwindling until the Kennedys realized that a reversal in three or four of the bigger states of the Midwest, Southwest and Far West could throw the election into the House of Representatives where unpledged electors from the Deep South would hold the balance of power.

Robert Kennedy's wife, Ethel, later described the atmosphere within the compound that day in these words: "We were happy, but uncertain. Bobby had that awful gnawing feeling that it could be reversed. No one else seemed as conscious of this as Bobby, Jack and Mr. Kennedy."

She added, however, that her husband was "much more tense about it than the others."

Despite his tenseness, Robert Kennedy—known to a whole nation as Bobby—led an assortment of male and female Kennedys onto the grass in front of his father's home for a brief forenoon go at the family sport, touch football. Senator Kennedy did not participate in the game, but did toss a football back and forth with Bobby in the early afternoon before he drove off to the Hyannis Armory to make a victory statement.

It is typical of the Kennedys that never once in public did they give a hint of the doubts that plagued them. While Republicans were charging vote fraud in Illinois and Texas and demanding recounts in other states, Senator Kennedy, exhibiting surface calm and assurance, moved ahead with plans for his administration.

When, on that day after the election, he first began considering some of the initial problems of the presidency and the change-over from the Eisenhower Administration to his own, Senator Kennedy turned for assistance to the same dedicated young man who had brilliantly organized and managed his campaign. This, of course, was Robert Kennedy.

Through much of the previous four year period, beginning almost immediately after Adlai E. Stevenson's overwhelming defeat in the 1956 presidential election, Robert Kennedy had devoted his amazing energies, his bright mind and his faculty for dispassionate decision to putting his brother in the White House.

There had been talk, both within the Kennedy organization and outside of it, that Robert Kennedy hankered for the Attorney Generalship. The rumor had been mentioned to both brothers, either seriously or in jest. But, said Robert after he had accepted the post, he and his brother never had discussed the matter prior to November 9, 1960.

As they lounged that day, both wearing slacks and sweaters, the discussion concerned recruitment of talent for "The New Frontier." The President-elect turned to the subject of his brother's future.

The Attorney General does not remember now exactly how his brother approached the subject or how he phrased the question. But he does remember that his brother was firm in wanting him to serve as Attorney General.

"I said I didn't think I was interested," reported Robert Kennedy later. "I had definitely decided I would take a rest to think over my future."

But the President-elect had become heavily dependent upon the judgment and devotion of his brother through two state-wide Senate elections in Massachusetts, three years together on the Senate Rackets Committee where John Kennedy was second ranking Democrat and Robert was chief counsel, and during the long fight for the Presidency. He persisted.

"He asked what else I would be interested in," said Robert Kennedy. "I said I didn't want to be in government."

The issue was dropped at that point. Two days later, the President-elect flew to Palm Beach, Florida, for a rest and to begin facing the monumental task of taking over leadership of the United States government from Dwight D. Eisenhower. Robert Kennedy and his effervescent wife, Ethel, headed for Acapulco, Mexico, accompanied by the youngest of the Kennedy brothers, Edward, and his wife, Joan.

For Robert Kennedy, this was a time to think about his own future.

His brother's proposal that he become fourth ranking member of the presidential cabinet was revolutionary even from a man who was the first Catholic, the youngest candidate and only the second member of the U. S. Senate to be elected President.

Although President Eisenhower had used his brother, Dr. Milton Eisenhower, in advisory posts and on goodwill missions, and President Franklin D. Roosevelt had employed his son, James, as his administrative

assistant in the White House, no previous president
had seriously considered bringing a member of his immediate family into his official family. President-elect
Kennedy, who won a Pulitzer Prize for his book on
American history, *Profiles in Courage,* and who was
knowledgeable about presidential history, was aware
a storm would break if he nominated Robert Kennedy
for Attorney General.

His opinion, stated privately to friends, was this:
He had seen situations like this before. An appointment is announced and a wave of criticism breaks.
Then the appointee gets the post, does a good job and
the criticism is forgotten. This is the way it would be
with his brother as Attorney General.

The President-elect was willing to undergo what he
expected to be "the most sensitive kind of criticism"
because he was convinced his brother was "the best
man I can get for the job."

But Robert Kennedy was not convinced.

On November 19, William H. Lawrence, writing for
The New York Times from Palm Beach, reported that
"President-elect John F. Kennedy is giving serious con-
sideration to the appointment of his younger brother
Robert as Attorney General."

In this first public mention of the President-elect's
plan, Lawrence said Senator Kennedy realized that
"some political criticism" might be generated if he
named his brother to the Cabinet. "But," wrote Lawrence, "Sen. Kennedy is known to feel that he should
not discriminate against his brother simply because of
the family relationship in view of Robert's record as
a lawyer."

Lawrence sought out the story after learning that
Governor Abraham Ribicoff of Connecticut was not
going to be Kennedy's Attorney General, as had been
reported. It is probable, however, that at the time Law-

rence obtained the information from his sources, Senator Kennedy was looking for a way to float a trial balloon on the projected appointment.

If this were his intent, the *Times* provided a quick reply of its own. In a November 23 editorial headlined MINISTRY OF TALENT, the *Times* threw back at Kennedy his campaign pledge that "all appointments, both high and low, will be made on the basis of ability—without regard to race, creed, national origin, sex, section or occupation."

To this, the *Times* added: "It is simply not good enough to name a bright young political manager, no matter how bright or how young or how personally loyal, to a major post in government that by rights (if not by precedent) ought to be kept completely out of the political arena."

The President-elect read the editorial at Palm Beach as he prepared to fly back to Washington to spend Thanksgiving Day, November 24, with his wife, Jacqueline, and his daughter, Caroline, who was just four days away from her third birthday. Although John Kennedy had written occasionally for the Sunday *Times Magazine* during his Senate days and had derived immeasurable political assistance from the same newspaper in the presidential campaign, the editorial did nothing to alter his view that Robert Kennedy should be Attorney General.

The telephone calls between Jack Kennedy and his brothers Robert and Edward, vacationing in Mexico, were frequent. Despite a temperamental Acapulco telephone system that only Edward seemed to be able to operate, the President-elect and Robert discussed government transitional problems a number of times. They talked about the search for talent, and the continuing question of whether it was possible for the election results to be overturned.

Robert Kennedy was still worried about the closeness of the vote, although Nixon had made it clear that he had no intention of contesting the outcome and actually recognized John Kennedy as the President-elect.

In Acapulco, Robert Kennedy also discussed his future with Ethel and his brother, Teddy. Ethel suggested he should do whatever he felt was the right thing, and that she would be bound by his decision.

Teddy, having determined not to take a post in his brother's administration, covered all the pitfalls of the problem with Robert and suggested that he continue to think it out. When Robert Kennedy arrived in Palm Beach for Thanksgiving, he still was opposed to becoming Attorney General.

The three Kennedy brothers had planned to meet in Palm Beach late Thanksgiving night in the ornate Spanish-style mansion owned by their father. Robert and Edward did arrive from Acapulco, but the stork stopped John Kennedy from keeping the rendezvous.

He flew from Washington to Palm Beach on Thanksgiving night. But the moment his twin-engine Convair, The *Caroline,* set down at Palm Beach International Airport, he learned by radio that Mrs. Kennedy had been rushed to Georgetown University Hospital in Washington. At the time he received the message, she already was undergoing a Caesarian section for delivery of her second child.

The worried President-elect immediately hurried aboard the four-engine plane that had brought news reporters to Palm Beach. He ordered a return flight to Washington. Shortly after the plane was airborne, Kennedy, standing in his shirt sleeves in the middle of the aisle, learned by radio that Mrs. Kennedy had been delivered of an infant son, John F. Kennedy, Jr.

The President-elect went directly from Washington National Airport to his wife's bedside. He decided to remain in Washington for a few weeks before returning to Palm Beach.

Robert and Ethel Kennedy stayed in Palm Beach for three days, returning to Washington on Sunday, November 27. They hurried to the President-elect's house and went with him to visit Mrs. Kennedy in the hospital.

During the next two weeks, the President-elect and Robert Kennedy were in constant touch with each other. The question of the appointment was raised occasionally; but even when it did not enter into the conversation between the two brothers, it was in both of their minds.

Both knew the time for a showdown was approaching. By mid-December, John Kennedy had publicly announced or at least privately selected almost his entire Cabinet. But Robert Kennedy remained adamant.

Old Joe Kennedy, watching from his fashionable Park Avenue apartment in New York, as his sons skirmished over the appointment, became concerned. "I don't know what's wrong with him," he said of Robert. "Jack needs all the good men he can get around him down there. There's none better than Bobby. You know, for six years he hasn't told me what he wants to do."

Joe Kennedy, for all his power and prestige in the family, was but a single pressure on Robert. Other pressures pushed in from all sides.

There was a movement afoot among his friends and some of John's to put him right at the President's elbow in the White House. But both men saw grave consequences in this. It would create a public impression that the President was too heavily dependent upon his younger brother. It also might have a tendency to isolate the President from the rest of his aides.

Fresh in the minds of both men were the problems

faced by President Eisenhower, who, because of his overreliance on Sherman Adams through the first six years of his administration, found himself handicapped when Adams was forced by the Goldfine scandal to resign.

Robert Kennedy also rejected suggestions that he accept appointment to John's Senate seat. "The only way I'll go to the Senate is run for it," he snapped, irate that anyone would think he would take the easy route.

He saw real challenges in the need to accelerate America's missile program and in the effort to gain lost prestige on the diplomatic front. He therefore seriously considered sub-Cabinet posts in the Defense and State departments.

A job in either area would have been quite a change for a young man who had built a reputation as a racket-buster and Communist-hunter. "I've been chasing bad guys all my life," he explained. "I'd like a change."

But he rejected both jobs when he realized that his presence in a sub-Cabinet post would create a difficult situation for the Cabinet officer he served under— either Secretary of State Dean Rusk or Secretary of Defense Robert S. McNamara. The feeling was that neither man would "want the President's little brother looking over his shoulder."

He fleetingly considered purchasing his own newspaper or preparing himself to take over the control of his father's financial empire. He debated whether to wait two years and run for Governor of Massachusetts.

To help him in his final determination, he sought counsel outside his family. He first went to the Department of Justice to ask Federal Bureau of Investigation Director J. Edgar Hoover if, as Attorney General, he could make a vigorous and effective fight against crime. Hoover said very emphatically that he could. Then he lunched on Capitol Hill with an old friend with whom he had once toured Russia, Associate Justice William O. Douglas. Although Robert Kennedy had not been in complete agreement with all of Douglas' rulings from the high bench in years past, he retained a warm personal regard and admiration for the Justice. For more than an hour he questioned Douglas and listened to his advice. Then he returned to the Department of Justice to talk with retiring Attorney General William Rogers about the job itself.

He had already discussed the matter with his old friend and mentor, Senator John McClellan of Arkansas. The box score was this: McClellan and Hoover advised him to become Attorney General, both insisting the job offered unlimited opportunities to benefit the nation. Although Justice Douglas agreed that Kennedy would make a fine Attorney General, he suggested that Robert consider a number of alternatives to benefit his career, including a college presidency. Kennedy had just about decided not to enter the Cabinet. "I knew that if I were going to do an effective job, I was going to be unpopular in some areas," he said in an April, 1961, *Look* magazine interview. "Everything I did would rub off on the President."

Still later, he confided: "I was never dying to be Attorney General."

After his meetings with Hoover, Douglas and Rogers, Robert drove to his white brick antebellum home, Hickory Hill, in McLean, Virginia, to ponder his decision. With him was John Seigenthaler, an able and daring *Nashville Tennessean* reporter who exposed Teamsters Union racketeering and hoodlumism in his home state and served as his assistant on the Democratic National Committee during the presidential campaign.

By the time darkness had fallen over the frozen,

snow-banked grounds of Hickory Hill, Robert Kennedy had firmly reached his decision. He telephoned the President-elect to tell him that he had decided to take a year's sabbatical to travel, write, and study—and not to be Attorney General. In this way, he felt he could prepare himself to step into the Administration at a later date.

But the man who had refused to take no for an answer when he was told that a forty-three-year-old Catholic Senator could not be elected President, refused also to take no for an answer when his brother said he would not become Attorney General.

"Let's talk it over at breakfast tomorrow," said John Kennedy. Robert Kennedy accepted the invitation.

During the eight-mile drive from McLean to Senator Kennedy's home the next morning, Robert Kennedy, with Seigenthaler at his side, did not utter three words. Immediately after he arrived at the red brick house at 3307 N Street Northwest in Georgetown, Robert Kennedy hurried upstairs for a private talk with his brother.

In a few minutes, the brothers came down together and breakfasted with Seigenthaler.

As they began to eat, Robert said to Jack: "Could we talk for a minute about what I'm going to do?"

The President-elect was ready for the question. "Let me just outline this thing for you," he said, grabbing the initiative.

John Kennedy was as superbly prepared for this persuasive argument as he had been for the television debates with Nixon that did so much to turn the election tide in his favor.

He made a direct appeal to his brother on a basis of duty and responsibility. He pointed out that he had asked a number of topflight business and professional men to enter his administration and they had agreed to do so at great personal sacrifice. He cited among others Dean Rusk, who was leaving the presidency of the Rockefeller Foundation; C. Douglas Dillon, who was giving up the chance to return to his great banking firm, and also turning his back on his own political party in agreeing to become Secretary of Treasury; and Adlai Stevenson, who had agreed to become United States Ambassador to the United Nations although he twice had been his party's presidential nominee.

John Kennedy emphasized that he expected complete loyalty from all of his Cabinet officers. But, he said, he did not really know a single member of the Cabinet personally, except for Health, Education and Welfare Secretary Abraham Ribicoff. He said he had leaned on his brother for advice in the past and needed to do so in the future.

The President-elect then launched into his clinching argument. He stressed that the job of Attorney General would be difficult, especially in the area of civil rights. But, he told his brother, if the administration was going to give the nation leadership, it had to have leaders. He concluded by stating that if all the others he had called upon had accepted, Robert, as his brother, could not refuse to serve.

Robert Kennedy sat silently for a few minutes at the table, his thin boyishly handsome face sober. He did not make a formal reply. He did not have to. He was going to be Attorney General.

The decision, however, was much broader than mere agreement to serve in his brother's Cabinet. It actually meant that when the chips were down, Robert Kennedy would serve anywhere in the Government where his brother felt he could do the most good.

With the ordeal of decision finally lifted from his shoulders, he indulged his sense of humor. He telephoned the President-elect that afternoon to suggest facetiously that John Kennedy should paraphrase Dwight D. Eisenhower's comment about Sherman Adams, and tell the press: "I know he's my brother, but I need him."

Also in a humorous vein, he later said that, in ignoring criticism from highly influential individuals and institutions: "Jack has the guts of a burglar."

The morning after the decision was made and the uncertainty was ended, John Kennedy stepped out onto the ice-encrusted steps of his town house to announce that Dillon would be Secretary of the Treasury and that J. Edward Day, the choice for Postmaster General, would meet with him in Palm Beach the next day.

Then, in a manner that was almost grave, he said that Robert F. Kennedy would be Attorney General.

"I have felt we should secure the best talent we could get for every position, regardless of party and regardless of any other factor," said the President-elect, "and I think that in every position this test has been applied, and has been applied in this case, to my satisfaction and, I hope, to the satisfaction of the Senate and the people of this country."

Criticism exploded immediately across the land. Even reporters standing in near-zero weather on N Street to cover the announcement got into an angry argument over the merits of the appointment.

Once again, *The New York Times* led the fight. "The one appointment thus far that we find most disappointing is Mr. Kennedy's choice of his young brother Robert as Attorney General," said the newspaper that had given such strong pre-election support to Kennedy that Nixon's camp had accused two of its reporters of exhibiting unfair political bias.

The *Times* added that Robert's experience as chief counsel for the McClellan Rackets Committee "is surely insufficient to warrant his appointment."

The New York *Daily News,* which bitterly opposed Kennedy's election, took a more philosophical approach.

"Brother Bob's appointment will be greeted with a squawk of 'nepotism' (a $3 word which means getting jobs for one's relatives) so Bob will have to be extraconscientious as head of the Justice Department if he is to justify his brother's selection of him," the *News* told its two million readers on December 17.

Although many Republicans openly criticized the appointment, Robert Kennedy faced only token opposition when he appeared at his confirmation hearing before the Senate Judiciary Committee on January 13, 1961.

Senator Everett McKinley Dirksen of Illinois, the Republican leader of the Senate and its last truly flamboyant orator, pursued briefly what he called the "historical departure" in appointing as Attorney General a man who never had had courtroom experience. But, in the end, he voted to confirm Robert Kennedy.

When the nomination moved to the Senate floor on January 21, the day after President Kennedy's inauguration, there was only one vote against it. That one was cast by Senator Gordon Allott, a Republican of Colorado, who told the Senate he could not "in conscience" vote to sustain the nomination of a man who was less qualified than thousands of other lawyers in the nation to be Attorney General.

About three hours after the Senate cast its vote, Robert Kennedy, nine other Cabinet officers and Ambassador Stevenson lined up at the south end of the great crystal-and-gold East Room of the White House to have Chief Justice Earl Warren administer their oath of office to them. Watching with pride were the new President, his elegant First Lady, Robert Kennedy's lovely wife Ethel, and nearly one dozen other members of the Clan Kennedy.

Chapter Two
"His Interest Is the Same as Mine"

As HIS FIRST YEAR IN THE WHITE HOUSE ENDED, JOHN F. Kennedy sat in his oval office discussing his unusual dual relationship with the man who is closer to him than any other, his brother and fourth-ranking Cabinet officer, Robert F. Kennedy.

Tracing both his professional and personal relationship with his brother, the President pointed out that prior to his successful 1952 Senate campaign against Henry Cabot Lodge he had not worked closely with him. Robert Kennedy's participation in Jack's 1946 Congressional primary fight was limited to three wards in East Cambridge and, as the President explained, he had little opportunity to display his abilities. But in 1952, Bob, then just twenty-six years old, proved himself to everyone involved in the Senatorial campaign, including his older brother.

"Bob has exceptional organizational talents," said the President. "My 1952 campaign was terribly disorganized. The man I had running it was having a breakdown and I was doing too much organizational work to campaign properly. Then Bobby came in. And there was a tremendous change in two or three weeks.

We had a lot of fights on our hands, but he got things organized and moving. He got people working in all of the counties. It was an exceptional job. It was the first time I ever saw Bobby operate."

The President recalled an incident from the campaign which since has been cited by both Robert Kennedy's foes and friends as an example of the nononsense single-mindedness and toughness he brings to any undertaking. Shortly after becoming manager of Jack's campaign, he discovered that the local politicians who wandered into headquarters, ostensibly to volunteer their services, actually wanted only to sit around and talk about the upcoming election and have their pictures taken at rallies. They also were unimpressed initially by the campaign manager, who looked like a bashful and unseasoned college boy lost in a cold political wilderness. Robert Kennedy may have been bashful and unseasoned, but he soon proved to the politicians that he was not lost. When a group sauntered into headquarters one day, Robert told them bluntly that if they wanted to work in the campaign they could begin by addressing and licking envelopes on the great volume of literature the Kennedy's were mailing out. The politicians left in a huff and did not return.

Eight years later, when he was managing his brother's preconvention presidential campaign, angry Democratic politicians again charged that Jack's little brother was treating them harshly. There were assertions that Robert was tough in forcing Ohio's Governor Michael V. DiSalle off the fence and into Jack Kennedy's camp and that he also dealt brusquely with Pennsylvania's Governor David Lawrence and California's Governor Edmund (Pat) Brown. The President, however, credits little substance to the charges.

"They always seemed nonsensical to me," said John

Kennedy. "Bobby had a terribly tough job to do. I used to hear stories about his ruthlessness and as to who he was ruthless with. But I never heard them documented. I never heard any evidence of it. He is tough about getting work done. I think those stories began with the incident in 1952 when the Boston politicians first came in and Bobby told them to write envelopes or get out."

The President pointed out that after the 1952 election, he and his brother did not become involved jointly in a major long-range project until the Senate Rackets Committee was formed in 1957, with Jack as a member and Robert as chief counsel under the chairmanship of Senator John McClellan. Robert Kennedy, of course, did take charge of his brother's brief, spectacular bid for the Democratic vice-presidential nomination in 1956. But that was a spur-of-the-moment operation that began and ended with the five-day Democratic national convention in Chicago.

"Bobby did a tremendous job on the McClellan Committee," President Kennedy declared. "He demonstrated his organizational abilities and his exceptional capacity for hard work. In the 1960 presidential campaign, he did the same thing. He had an awfully exceptional organization operating in 1960."

John Kennedy then turned to the present and discussed what it means to him to have his brother in his Cabinet as Attorney General and also as troubleshooter and adviser for a vast range of problems not directly associated with the Attorney Generalship.

"In the first place, his judgment is good and his interest is the same as mine," said the President. "He has ideas and the ability to turn ideas into action. This is a rare quality. Some people have good ideas but are unable to turn them into action. There are a lot of things that we never really get into together. But there are other things I talk to him about. Most of the time, his views and mine are in accordance. But there have been one or two times when he held different views from mine."

The President emphasized the importance of the "community of interest" that his brother shares with him. He suggested that Robert Kennedy instinctively acts to nurture that interest because of "his sense of being my brother and because he has worked for me for a long period of time."

Robert Kennedy's manifold activities on behalf of the President in his first year and a half as Attorney General carried him far afield from the confines of the Department of Justice and spread his influence through much of the United States Government.

When the high hopes for the rebel invasion of Cuba in April, 1961, dissolved into a tragic, shattered dream, the President ordered a thorough investigation of the nation's intelligence network. He brought General Maxwell D. Taylor out of retirement to head up the job, but also assigned Admiral Arleigh Burke, the Chief of Naval Operations, and the Attorney General to work on the arduous two-month study.

When the President himself was unable to accept an invitation to attend the first anniversary celebraion of the independence of the Ivory Coast Republic, he sent Robert Kennedy as his personal ambassador.

In the earliest days on the New Frontier, the President enlisted the aid of his brother to help break the hold that a conservative coalition of Republicans and Southern Democrats held on the Rules Committee, which clears all legislation for action on the floor of the House of Representatives.

When the President launched a nationwide series of regional conferences to inform the people about his administration's policies and progress in the fall of

1961, he sent the Attorney General to Chicago to keynote the meetings which were staged in the major cities of the nation with Vice President Lyndon Johnson, six other Cabinet members and a variety of top government officials participating.

The Attorney General was able on the "Meet the Press" television program of September 24, 1961, to inform both the American people and the Kremlin's leaders that there was "no question" that President Kennedy was ready to use nuclear weapons to defend West Berlin. "If it comes to that," declared Robert Kennedy, "he will use nuclear weapons."

When he and his wife, Ethel, went to Newport News, Virginia, July 15, 1961, to launch the Polaris missile submarine *John Marshall,* the Attorney General spoke for the Kennedy Administration in warning Soviet Premier Nikita Khrushchev not to make Adolf Hitler's mistake of "underestimating the American people." He stated that although Americans wanted peace, they "are a tough, viable, industrious people who will tend to their responsibilities in this climactic time in world affairs."

In mid-1961, the President assigned the Attorney General to a long-continuing study to determine how America can improve its psychological warfare position against the Soviet Union.

The day before the President began a pre-Thanksgiving Day tour of the Western United States to warn against the "discordant voices" of the far right, the Attorney General sounded a similar alarm in Dallas, Texas, a stronghold of super-conservatism. "I have no sympathy with those who are defeatists and who would rather be 'red than dead,' " said the Attorney General, "nor do I have sympathy with those, who in the name of fighting communism, sow seeds of suspicion and distrust by making false or irresponsible charges, not only against their neighbors, but against courageous teachers and public officials and against the foundations of our government—Congress, the Supreme Court and even the Presidency itself. As a vigilant, experienced American who has real credentials as a Communist fighter—J. Edgar Hoover—has said, such actions play into Communist hands and hinder, rather than aid, the fight against communism." Taking note of the ludicrous charge by John Birch Society President Robert Welch that Dwight D. Eisenhower was "a conscious agent of the Communist party," Robert Kennedy quipped: "The only Communist the John Birchers have uncovered is President Eisenhower."

The Attorney General provoked criticism for himself and his brother in the sensitive, race-conscious South—where at least one newspaper called him the Richelieu of the New Frontier—by forecasting on a Voice of America broadcast that a Negro could become President "in the foreseeable future."

At the beginning of his second year in the Cabinet, Robert Kennedy's activities on behalf of his older brother carried him on a global tour that gave him new stature as a well-schooled, hard-working diplomat with a particular flair for dealing successfully on a people-to-people basis.

Reaction both at home and abroad to the travels of Robert and Ethel Kennedy in February, 1962, generally was admiring, although the journey was criticized by some columnists—particularly Henry J. Taylor—and produced a new crop of remarks about the "Kennedy dynasty" attempting to perpetuate itself. One of the most favorable evaluations, however, came from former Vice President Richard M. Nixon, whose 1960 presidential ambitions Robert Kennedy helped shatter.

The trip was built around the Attorney General's acceptance of an invitation from West Berlin Mayor

Willy Brandt to visit that beleagured city and make the Ernst Reuter Memorial Address honoring Brandt's late predecessor. Once the President's personable and powerful brother was scheduled to go abroad, country after country asked to see him, and he obliged by expanding the trip to include visits to Japan, India, Pakistan, Indonesia, Thailand, Italy, South Vietnam, Hong Kong, West Germany, the Netherlands and France.

The Kremlin even put out unofficial feelers to Robert Kennedy to stop off for a visit with Nikita Khrushchev. The move was made at a time when Khrushchev was locked in political battle with the old Stalinists at home and in China and Albania, and when he also was pressuring for a summit meeting with the President and British Prime Minister Sir Harold Macmillan. There were various false reports that Robert Kennedy would end his tour in Moscow, but he and his brother decided against the Attorney General visiting Russia at that time.

The journey of American goodwill missionaries Robert and Ethel Kennedy was crowded with excitement. Their plane was delayed on its Los Angeles-Honolulu flight when it hit a bird. In Honolulu, they were spilled into the Pacific when a Navy dinghy upset. A mild earthquake jarred Tokyo during their visit in Japan. Several times the Kennedys were surrounded by mobs of hecklers, and they even were splattered with eggs.

President Kennedy later emphasized that one of the major reasons for sending his brother abroad was to have Robert Kennedy, himself young and vigorous, talk to students who hate the United States largely because they misunderstand it. The Attorney General debated the merits of democracy with some of the students even when he was in physical danger. The influential Japanese newspaper, *Y'omiuri Shimbun,* commented that the Attorney General demonstrated "a new diplomatic technique more effective than printing one million propaganda pamphlets."

The European end of the tour was less tumultuous and fitted more nearly into the traditional diplomatic mold. The Kennedys called upon Pope John XXIII while in Rome. The Attorney General told worried West Berliners that the United States would not abandon them to the Communists. He visited Queen Juliana in the Netherlands, and delivered a message from the President to President Charles De Gaulle in Paris.

In a report on the journey, *Time* magazine said Robert Kennedy "displayed all the qualities that have made him ... a major power in the United States Government ... the kid brother is one of the President's solidest assets."

Nixon, appearing on nationwide television, stated that the Attorney General "has many of the qualifications that would make him a very effective leader in the field of foreign policy. He's tough-minded, he's quick, he's intelligent. He is one who has a tremendous will to win."

Other Republicans were less kind, and Texans generally exploded in ire at Robert Kennedy's statement to students of the University of Indonesia that the United States had made mistakes in the past, including the "unjustified" Mexican War.

In April, 1962, when the steel industry, led by United States Steel, announced a price increase of $6 a ton, President Kennedy angrily denounced the action as ruthless, irresponsible and contemptuous of the public interest. He immediately marshaled the dynamic forces of the Government to halt the price hike—and one of the most powerful of those forces was Robert Kennedy's Justice Department which launched an antitrust investigation into possible collusion by the steel firms in boosting their prices simultaneously. Within seventy-two hours the steel industry capitulated and announced it would not put the price boost into effect.

While the steel dispute was at boiling point, however, Federal Bureau of Investigation agents roused three newspaper reporters out of bed in the pre-dawn hours to question them about an alleged statement by the president of the Bethlehem Steel Corporation that the price increase was not necessary. When news of the incident got out, Robert Kennedy was charged with utilizing police-state tactics to gain information about the steel industry.

The President had asked his brother to find out for him what the Bethlehem executive had said, and the Attorney General, in turn, called upon the FBI to carry out the task. But, Robert Kennedy's aides explained later, the Attorney General did not mean for the FBI agents to get reporters out of bed. Nevertheless, Robert Kennedy took full responsibility for the incident.

A few months earlier, when the Berlin crisis appeared to be catapulting East and West each day closer to the brink of war, the Attorney General met privately with Soviet Ambassador Mikhail A. Menshikov to discuss this tense situation and other disputes between the Communist and free worlds. This session so disturbed Representative John V. Lindsay, a liberal New York Republican, that he wrote a letter to Secretary of State Dean Rusk protesting it. He stated, in part, that the Kennedy-Menshikov conference "bypasses your office and your Department, and in so doing runs great risks" and that it also was "part of a growing pattern" of foreign relations being conducted in a casual manner by "personalities untrained in foreign policy and the art of diplomacy."

Rusk replied: "It is, as you know, a general practice for high officials of the Government to meet with ambassadors of foreign governments. This is a time-honored and traditional practice and a matter to which we ourselves attach the greatest importance as our own ambassadors abroad carry out their heavy responsibilities.

"In Washington it is not at all unusual for foreign ambassadors to call upon members of the Senate or the House of Representatives, even though ambassadors are officially credited to the President. Both here and abroad such contacts are expected to be governed by canons of judgment and good taste. In the particular instance to which you referred in your letter, the Attorney General and I discussed this request for an appointment before it was granted to the Soviet Ambassador and discussed the topics which might be expected to come up.

"Subsequently the Attorney General and I discussed what had been said. There could not be any objection, therefore, on the grounds that there was any lack of co-ordination with those primarily responsible for the conduct of our foreign relations.

"As a matter of practice, all members of the Cabinet, as well as other high officials of the Government, keep the State Department fully informed with regard to matters of significance that may arise in their talks with foreign diplomats."

Lindsay contended that Rusk's letter did not answer his basic objection that the Attorney General, without training in foreign policy but as the authorized spokesman for the President, discussed sensitive, highly explosive matters, including Berlin, in private with the Soviet Ambassador.

The Attorney General's own reaction to Lindsay's protest was that it was "childish." His response, during an interview, was this question: "Doesn't he have anything else to do? As long as I'm getting my job done as Attorney General," he added, "what I do with the rest of my time and what my relationship with my brother might be is my business."

President Kennedy, continuing the interview in his office, said he thought Rusk's reply "demolished" Lindsay's argument. And like his younger brother, the President asked a question: "Doesn't the Attorney General of the United States have the right to talk to the Soviet Ambassador?"

"Let me see if I can categorize the areas we might talk about," said the President, thinking over the various governmental matters in which Robert Kennedy has been interested.

"He has sat in on the talks about Berlin and Germany, but he doesn't participate in the discussion," said the President. "He also sits in on the National Security Council. But there are some matters that interest him and some that don't. He is too busy running his own Department to bother himself with matters that don't interest him. I would not, for instance, discuss the international trade problem with him. He is interested in the Dominican Republic and the whole Caribbean security problem. He also is interested in South Vietnam. The psychological warfare study was his interest. He suggested it. I think one of our great problems is getting our agencies—the State Department, the CIA, the USIA, the Pentagon—co-ordinated and stabilized on this psychological warfare problem. Bobby's study has been helpful, but it is a continuing matter and he will continue to study it."

Both Kennedys have been disturbed by America's disadvantage in the area of psychological and political influence. They noted when the Communists raised their wall between East and West Berlin and when they renewed atmospheric testing of nuclear weapons, it drew little criticism around the world. "If the United States had ever taken any action such as that you would have heard about it everywhere," said Robert Kennedy. "There would have been bombs thrown, there would have been flags hauled down in front of our USIA headquarters, windows would have been broken."

The President was asked, as he sat in his rocking chair on that lovely winter afternoon, whether he depended more on his brother in the earliest days of his administration, when many of his Cabinet officers still were strangers to him, than he does now. "No," replied John Kennedy. "It's about the same now as in the beginning." But he added that the longer he works with those who have joined him at the summit of the New Frontier, the more able he is to talk confidentially with them as he does with Bob.

During the fateful week before anti-Castro forces launched their predawn invasion at Cuba's Bahia de Cochinos (Bay of Pigs) on April 17, 1961, the President discussed the multifold dangers of the operation with his brother. The Attorney General approved the invasion.

"I felt, based on the facts that were presented to the President," Robert Kennedy later explained, "that it was a worthwhile venture. And, I dare say, if the same facts were presented to him again, he would reach the same conclusion. Any reasonable man would make the same decision. You make a decision based on fact."

Robert Kennedy was making a speech in colonial Williamsburg, Virginia, on that unhappy Monday when the Cuban rebels attempted to establish a foothold on the shores of their tropical homeland. When the President realized that the invasion was headed for disaster, he telephoned his brother in Williamsburg and said: "Why don't you come home and let's discuss it."

Robert Kennedy flew back to Washington that afternoon and immediately became an active and forceful participant in an almost constant round of White House conferences concerning the Cuban tragedy. After the last hopes had faded for a successful coup against Fidel Castro, there remained the overpowering question of how to avoid such debacles in the future.

The discussions that transpired between the President and his brother are secret. Robert Kennedy will not disclose what views he expressed or what particular recommendations he made to the President. But as a result of the White House post-mortems over Cuba, John Kennedy realigned top personnel both in the Executive Mansion and the Department of State. He also determined that there was urgent need for a re-evaluation of America's intelligence apparatus so that he would not be forced again to make a major decision based on information that might prove misleading or false. The President summoned General Maxwell D. Taylor out of retirement to head the study and assigned his brother, Robert, as one of three men to assist in it.

"I realized if he was there, he would give Max Taylor additional force," explained the President in the interview. "He would show that there was no interest in who was to blame—the White House, the CIA, the State Department. We wanted to find out what was wrong and what could be done."

The Chief Executive then came to a discussion of the responsibilities and loneliness of his office and whether these burdens have been eased by the presence in his administration of a devoted and talented brother who

usually talks with him in person or on the telephone
at least once each day.

"No one can take the burden of responsibility," explained the President. "Others can advise you, but you
have to make the ultimate decisions. It is very difficult
to find someone you have regard for, someone who has
the same interest. My interest is in having this thing
work well. Of course, we all have that interest. But
Bobby also is my brother, and therefore I'm closer to
him than to others. Bobby sets a high standard for himself. He has a sense of responsibility for himself, for
his own family and for the whole [Kennedy] family
that is rather highly developed."

Finally, the President was asked whether he was concerned over the claim that Bob had spent too much of
his life in his older brother's shadow. John Kennedy
said he did not think this was true. He said he did not
believe that in their lengthy service together "Bobby
ever has had to submerge himself."

When Joseph P. Kennedy bowed out as chairman of
of the National Maritime Commission during the New
Deal, Franklin D. Roosevelt wrote him a personal note
saying:

> Dear Joe:
> You have maintained your justly earned repu-
> tation of being a two-fisted, hard-hitting executive.

When Robert Kennedy ends his tenure on the New
Frontier, John Kennedy justifiably could write the same
message to his brother. But to it he could add the words
that explain better than any others why Bob Kennedy
is an influence second only to the Chief Executive himself in the current administration: "Your interest has
been mine."

Chapter Three
What Makes Bobby Run

"BOBBY KENNEDY HAS TO BE FIRST ALL THE TIME." ✳
In these nine words, David Powers, the genial official greeter of the White House and a long-time political lieutenant of John F. Kennedy, gives his assessment of the drive that motivates the President's brother
and has made him, in his middle thirties, the second
most powerful man in the Government of the United
States.

Powers, whose balding head is crammed with colorful anecdotes about baseball and politics, states his
view with admiration not deprecation. He sees Robert
Kennedy as a man cut in the dynamic mold of the
great Ty Cobb. In fact, Powers summons a memorable
story about the Georgia Peach from baseball's past to
illustrate his meaning. It concerns the era just after
the turn of the century when Cobb was eighteen years
old, playing for Augusta in the old Sally League and
rooming with a good-natured pitcher named Nap
Rucker.

In those days it was the practice for players to dress
in their uniforms in their hotel rooms before going to
the ball park. Cobb and Rucker did this, but after
each game Cobb rushed back to the hotel and always
was first into the bathtub. One day when Rucker was
knocked out of a game in the seventh inning, however,
the pitcher wandered back to the room ahead of Cobb
and leisurely immersed himself in a tub of warm

water. While he was bathing, Cobb burst in upon him in a fiery rage. The furious Georgia Peach first hurled insults at Rucker and then lunged at him. Freeing himself from Cobb's hold, the incredulous pitcher demanded to know why Cobb was acting so maniacal just because "I was first in the tub today—and for the first time, too."

"Don't you understand, Nap?" pleaded Cobb, trying desperately to explain a compulsion beyond his control. "I've just got to be first—all the time."

"Bobby Kennedy is like that," says Powers, who has known both Kennedy brothers since 1946. "He's got to be first all the time."

Yet he is not a man obsessed with first place for himself alone. He is possessed of a devotion and loyalty to others, especially his older brother, that would appear to contradict Powers's analysis. In a profile on the Attorney General in *The Kennedy Circle,* Hugh Sidey writes:

> If there is one consistent theme in the life of Robert Kennedy over his 35 years, it is the fact that he seems to have been working for someone else, that he has lived in a shadow. He has been distinguished in his own right, for certain, but others—particularly Jack—have gained as much from his inexhaustible energy. So it is now. He is once again at his brother's side, this time working for the success of the New Frontier.

How, then, can a man driven ever toward the top, compromise for a niche just short of the top? The answer lies in the unique relationship of the Brothers Kennedy. These two young men are such a superbly co-ordinated unit that between them there actually is no first and no second. What one attains, the other attains. What one loses, the other loses. In the annals of American politics, there is no comparable relationship of one brother to another.

Together John and Robert Kennedy have undertaken four major public ventures—John Kennedy's 1952 senatorial campaign and his 1960 presidential race; the Senate Rackets Committee investigation; and now the development and operation of the New Frontier. In only one of these endeavors, the rackets probe, has Robert Kennedy had the occasional opportunity to step out of his brother's shadow and into a spotlight where he could display his own abilities, divorced from concern over the political success or failure of John Kennedy. There have been times, as in the month before he agreed to become Attorney General, that Robert Kennedy has pondered the possibility of setting out wholly on his own. But his sense of duty and dedication each time has directed him back onto the path trod by his brother.

Indicative of this dual drive in the Attorney General's life is an incident that occurred in 1957, just one year after John Kennedy had lost the Democratic Vice-Presidential nomination to Estes Kefauver and at a time when Robert Kennedy and his televised inquiry into labor-management misdoings were the talk of the nation.

James Riddle Hoffa, the pugnacious teamster, was tried that summer on charges of attempting to bribe one of Robert Kennedy's investigators, John Cye Cheasty, into furnishing him secret information from the Committee's files. Seldom has Robert Kennedy been as emotionally involved as he was in this case. Not only was he personally convinced that Hoffa was guilty of grievous legal and moral wrongs, but more and more he was coming to see Hoffa as the man of greatest evil in the American labor movement. Kennedy was so confident that the Government would win the case against Hoffa that he stated brashly he would "jump off the Capitol" if Hoffa were acquitted.

But he had not reckoned with the prospect that the Government would go into court with its case carelessly and ineffectively prepared. Nor had he counted on the brilliance and the cunning of the defense, led by Edward Bennett Williams, one of the nation's most prominent criminal lawyers. Eight of the twelve jurors were Negroes, and Williams attempted in every conceivable manner to influence them from a racial as well as a legal point of view. He brought two Negro attorneys in to aid him, ran former Heavyweight Champion Joe Louis into the courtroom to embrace Hoffa, attempted to show that John Cye Cheasty had once investigated the National Association for the Advancement of Colored People, and posed with a Negro woman lawyer, Martha Jefferson, for an ad in the *Afro-American* praising Hoffa as a friend of the Negro. When Hoffa took the stand to testify, the Government prosecutors were unprepared to cross-examine him.

Hoffa was acquitted. Kennedy did not jump. But, in the quiet of his office, he told a reporter a few days later: "The two greatest disappointments of my life have been my brother's losing the vice-presidential nomination and the acquittal of Jimmy Hoffa."

Although Robert Kennedy has walked in his brother's shadow, he has done so as a partner and not as a servant. In each of his undertakings with his brother, he has had his own autonomous domain—an area in which he was number one—where he could make decisions, issue orders, run a large staff and occasionally argue policy with John Kennedy. He is in full command at the Department of Justice. John Kennedy also has made him as complete a partner as any man can be with the President of the United States in the operation of the Federal Government.

"Bobby is first because the President is first," says Dave Powers. "He is first in his field, and within the family it doesn't count. He's first in Jack's needs, first in Jack's confidence, first in Jack's wants."

What Powers describes as the urge to be first, others who have known and worked with Robert Kennedy over the years define in different words and with less dramatic analogies. But it all comes out the same: He instinctively is David, bent upon slaying any Goliath that rises before him.

One of John Kennedy's earliest recollections of his younger brother involves this almost fanatical determination to master the task before him against all odds.

Bobby was about four years old at the time and could not swim. Yet when his older brothers and sisters took him sailing in a yawl on Nantucket Sound, he jumped into the chill, deep waters over and over again, resolved to swim or drown in the attempt. He did not drown because his oldest brother, Joe, Jr., was swimming nearby. Looking back on the incident, John Kennedy wryly remarks: "It showed either a lot of guts or no sense at all, depending on how you looked at it."

Kenneth O'Donnell, who now acts as President Kennedy's appointments secretary and as something of a political trouble-shooter for the White House, noted the same stubborn tenacity in Robert Kennedy at Harvard.

The two had met in 1945 when Bob was sent to the university of his father and his brothers as a Navy V-12 officer trainee. When they returned in the fall of 1946, Bob and Ken became close personal friends, although they were not roommates as has been reported.

"I had no idea who he was when we first met in

1945," says O'Donnell, the son of a college football coach. "I was from Worcester, and, difficult as it may be to believe now, the Kennedys were unknown in Massachusetts [as differentiated from Boston] politics."

The major impression Robert made on O'Donnell and his football teammates was that he was a tough, friendly little guy who was determined to be a star on the gridiron despite his lack of weight and height. They did not realize that he was the son of an illustrious family until one day the *Boston Post* printed a story, headlined: AMBASSADOR KENNEDY'S SON STARS IN SCRIMMAGE.

Robert Kennedy and Ken O'Donnell were drawn together by a common misery: They were the only members of the varsity football team who were not berthed in the varsity locker room. Ken, who later was captain of the team, was left out of the locker room because of his belated enrollment. Bob was left out because he had been playing fourth string.

O'Donnell recalls: "We would eat together and complain together." At that juncture in his life, football was the world Kennedy was set to conquer and since O'Donnell was a skilled gridiron performer, he enlisted Ken to teach him how to toss and receive passes. Ken O'Donnell says Bob would arrive an hour earlier than other team members and stay an hour later.

Kennedy had "no right to be on the varsity team" because of his small size and inexperience, explains O'Donnell, but he made it strictly on determination. O'Donnell describes Kennedy on the football field as "A quick, tough guy who worked five times as hard as anybody and would charge in from his end of the line like a wild Indian, like a shot from a cannon."

Although he was the shortest, lightest and least coordinated of the four Kennedy boys, Robert is the only one who realized the family ambition of making his football letter in the Harvard-Yale game. He accomplished the feat in 1947 by playing right end with a fractured leg in a cast.

"The major difference between Bobby and his brothers," explains Ethel Kennedy, "is that Bobby always had to fight for everything."

K. LeMoyne Billings, who had been a close personal friend of all the Kennedys since he was Jack's roommate at Choate School, agrees with this evaluation. He says: "Teddy and Jack are much more alike in their natural attributes. Jack always has been a good public speaker. The same is true for Teddy. Both are very natural and easy in their dealings with other people. But for Bobby speaking and dealing with people has been difficult. Everything has come much harder for Bobby. He has to work harder."

Billings also is in basic agreement with Dave Powers's assessment of the propelling force in Robert Kennedy's life—that he must be in full command of whatever domain falls within his jurisdiction.

Lem had known Robert Kennedy more than a decade when they tackled their first working project together in Jack Kennedy's initial bid for a seat in Congress. Since Jack was seeking election from the 11th District of Massachusetts, which never has elected a Republican, the real battleground was the primary in the early summer of 1946.

Jack had nine opponents, but by far the most threatening one was Michael J. Neville, who as mayor of Cambridge could be expected to carry a very large vote in a key sector of the congressional district. Billings was placed in charge of Cambridge, but Robert was given three wards in East Cambridge.

"As I recall it," says Billings, "he established his own headquarters and let me know that this was his area. He had three wards out of the eleven in my jurisdiction. He handled them 100 per cent and he didn't want me to even show up there."

When the campaign ended with Jack Kennedy the victor over his nine opponents, Bob, who was just twenty-one, and Lem went off for a trek through Latin America. While in Chile they visited a ski resort and there Robert saw a high mountain that he decided needed to be climbed. He and Billings started toward the summit early in the day, but Lem gave out halfway up. Others who had visions of conquering the mountain also turned back short of the top. "But Bobby never stopped," says Lem. "He spent all day and got to the top. This sums up Bobby Kennedy: If he decides in his mind he's going to do something, nothing will stop him."

But the Attorney General is not just cold, tough determination on one hand and selfless devotion to his brother on the other. There are delicate shadings within his personality and some fascinating cross currents. He is the inheritor of much of Joseph P. Kennedy's brusque brilliance and resourceful aggressiveness. He also is the inheritor of Rose Kennedy's deep religious faith and gentle thoughtfulness. He is the inheritor from both parents of a great love of family.

Although he has achieved goals beyond the reach of most men his age, he has moved from one step to another in his brief and spectacular career with a sort of uncharted aimlessness. He has followed no grand design for self-accomplishment. In every period of his life he seems honestly not to have known where he wanted to go next.

When Robert Kennedy was graduated from Harvard in 1948, he enrolled in the University of Virginia Law School because, as he explains it, "I just didn't know anything when I got out of college. I wanted to do graduate work, but I didn't know whether to go to law school or business school. I had no attraction to business, so I entered law school."

By somewhat the same happenstance, he became an attorney in the criminal division of the Department of Justice after getting his law degree in 1951. Although he was interviewed by a big New York law firm, he took the post at Justice simply because he "wanted to go into the government."

Some romanticists have suggested that as a young lawyer in the Department, Robert Kennedy developed an intense desire to become Attorney General one day. He denies this. Recalling that era in his life, he says: "I had no interest in being Attorney General."

It was on the advice of two eminent lawyers that he first associated himself with Senator Joseph R. McCarthy's Permanent Investigations Subcommittee at the beginning of 1953. One was Francis (Frip) Flanagan, the panel's general counsel, and the other was then-Assistant Attorney General James McInerney. It was on the suggestion of Clark Mollenhoff, a Pulitzer Prize winning reporter for the *Des Moines Register and Tribune,* that Kennedy embarked on the Teamster Union probe that made him a national figure overnight.

Robert Kennedy has conquered each mountain he set out to climb, but almost invariably he has stumbled onto the trail at the beginning of the ascent.

One of his earliest roadblocks was an incendiary temper. He still has it, but has made impressive strides toward controlling its eruptions. Kenneth O'Donnell noticed when he began working with him on the Rackets Committee in 1957 that he was a more mature and less explosive individual than he had been in college or even in the 1952 senatorial campaign. "That was the biggest change I saw in Bob," says O'Donnell. "He had matured."

One who watched this change take form was Ruth Watt, a charming lady from New England who was chief clerk for the two Senate committees that Robert Kennedy served from 1953 through 1959. "Miss Ruth," as Senator John McClellan has called her for many years, recalls that he had many a struggle within himself to contain his temper. When he did blow up at an employee, Mrs. Watt remembers, he always apologized later.

The impression Kennedy left with Mrs. Watt was that of a thoughtful, energetic young man who hired employees because of their abilities and experience and not because of their political affiliation, and who was capable of the kindest gestures.

On Good Friday he sent orchids to all the girls in his office. At Christmas time he entertained the entire staff with a dinner at his home. He joined enthusiastically in celebrating minor milestones in the lives of his employees. When the committee finally ended its work, he made sure that everyone had a job.

Religion always has been a vital force in Robert Kennedy's life and seems to govern the moral and ethical tone of his existence. For years he has had a mass celebrated each year on the anniversary of the death of his sister Kathleen, his beloved "Kick," who was killed in a 1948 airplane crash. On his first trip to Europe after the war, he visited the grave of William J. R. Cavendish, the Marquess of Hartington, Kathleen's aristocratic husband who died heroically in combat in France. After his pilgrimage to the grave of Billy Hartington, he wrote a letter to Hartington's mother, the Duchess of Devonshire, describing his visit.

In the fall of 1961, Robert Kennedy provided the greatest thrill in the life of Charles Nichols, an elderly

Negro who was retiring after nearly two decades in the Justice Department. The Attorney General summoned the faithful employee to his office for a farewell ceremony and then asked him: "You're going to the White House, aren't you?" Nichols looked at him with incredulity written across his weathered face. The Attorney General quickly explained that President and Mrs. Kennedy were entertaining the Judiciary and officials of the Justice Department that night and had asked the long-time employee to attend. Furthermore Robert Kennedy had a car waiting to drive Nichols home so that he could dress for the White House party. It was a night the old gentleman never will forget.

The Attorney General has a particular interest in young people and delights in having students visit his office. In the spring of 1961, he once stood on his desk for a half hour answering questions posed by about a hundred Negro orphans. In January 1962, he cooked hamburgers in his office fireplace for a huge group of offspring of Justice Department officials and members of Congress.

It is one of the contradictions of Robert Kennedy's personality that he can exhibit such sensitivity toward the emotions of others and then, in the words of one friend, suddenly "be rough and rude and sometimes hurt your feelings intentionally."

The roughness and the rudeness are innate to the pragmatism that Kennedy himself summed up shortly after he became Attorney General. Meeting with a group of U. S. attorneys, he said: "It doesn't matter if I hurt your feelings. It doesn't matter if you hurt my feelings. The important thing is to get the job done."

One friend, who has watched Kennedy grow since his days with Joe McCarthy, describes him this way: "He's honest. He's got a hell of a lot of energy and when he gets on the right track he's a persistent SOB who never lets up. His weakest point is that he is personally kind of disorganized, but he always has somebody around who can pick up the pieces. He's inclined to be impetuous and unreasonable on some things."

If this appraisal, by a man who is as bluntly honest and persistent as Kennedy himself, seems harsh, it is also quite a tribute to the Attorney General's ability to surround himself with men of talent. Bob's irritability and occasional arrogance normally would tend to make yes-men of his subordinates. Yet he has nothing but contempt for spineless individuals and, fortunately for himself and the Government, he gathered about him at the Justice Department a group of strong, independent-minded men.

Chief among these men of talent was Byron R. White, the superbly co-ordinated "Whizzer" of the gridiron two decades ago, who was Deputy Attorney General through the first fourteen months that Kennedy was Attorney General. White so brilliantly proved himself to the President and the Attorney General that John Kennedy elevated him to the Supreme Court to succeed retiring Justice Charles E. Whittaker. Between White and Robert Kennedy there is a strong bond of friendship and admiration. White, a Rhodes Scholar, football star and distinguished lawyer, turned down other high government posts, including Secretary of the Army, to serve with Robert Kennedy at Justice. He seemed to be the eventual likely successor to the Attorney General until the President decided that he had the proper qualities—and undoubtedly the proper political views—to fill the first Supreme Court vacancy of the Kennedy Administration.

Although White had met John Kennedy at Oxford University in Great Britain before World War II, he *integrity.*

did not meet Robert Kennedy until the spring of 1960 when Robert went to Colorado Springs to make a speech.

The former All-American football player, then a Denver attorney, was interested in the presidential bid of his old acquaintance, John F. Kennedy, and he and Robert discussed this on a ride from Colorado Springs to Denver. Not only did White's enthusiasm for John Kennedy grow during the visit, but he also was impressed with Robert Kennedy. "I thought he was a very well put together young fellow," says the tall Westerner whom the Attorney General, in his high-pitched Boston accent, occasionally calls "Whizzah."

After months of serving as Robert Kennedy's number-two man in the Justice Department, White was even more sold on him than he had been in the presidential campaign when they worked closely together.

"I think Bob is a very dedicated guy," said White in an interview. "He's got a lot of courage. He certainly tries to figure out what's right and wrong. He's got a very practical point of view about what can be done and what cannot be done. I think he feels that people aren't put on this earth just for looking-around purposes—just for pleasure. He wants to get things done. When he makes up his mind as to what he thinks is in the public interest, he's for it—win, lose or draw."

White then used the word that almost every friend and admirer resorts to in discussing Robert Kennedy—"integrity." "He believes in personal integrity and doing a job," explained the then Deputy Attorney General. "The obligations and requirements of the job take precedence over personal feelings."

One liability that other friends and all foes notice in Kennedy's make-up is his tendency to evaluate people in terms of blacks and whites. If you're for the Kennedys, you are a good guy. If you're against them, you are a bad guy. In his Rackets Committee days, the blacks included Jimmy Hoffa, the Kohler Company's Lyman C. Conger, and Chicago middleman Nathan Shefferman. Among the whites were the United Auto Workers' Walter Reuther, the Steelworkers' Arthur Goldberg (now Secretary of Labor) and "Big Jim" Elkins of Portland, Oregon, who exposed a three-way tie-up between the underworld, the Teamsters Union and leading Oregon politicians.

For all his inclination to choose sides unreasonably and to pursue a goal ruthlessly, Robert Kennedy is a man of awesome integrity. He likewise is extremely loyal to those he feels deserve his loyalty. "If I were ever in important trouble in my life," says Lem Billings, "Bobby would be the first person I'd go to. He is the most dependable guy and a terrific friend."

Hugh Sidey, in *The Kennedy Circle*, quotes one of Robert Kennedy's assistants as stating that he "is more concerned with morality and personal integrity than anybody I know. He doesn't like compromise."

Kennedy also despises hypocrisy. Shortly after he became Attorney General, he discovered there were only ten Negroes among the 950 lawyers employed by the Department of Justice. He immediately summoned Charles Smith, a Negro lawyer from Seattle, to work in the Department and began adding other Negroes to the staff. Kennedy had known Smith, had been impressed with his work on a Seattle case involving ex-Teamsters President Dave Beck, and had felt that he would be a wise addition to the Department. So, by hiring Smith, he was able to bring into his Department a man who was both an able lawyer and a prominent Negro. To his assistant, John Seigenthaler, he explained: "How can we go out into the field and tell people to put

Negroes in school and let Negroes ride buses if we don't have Negroes in here?"

Likewise, in September, 1961, the President's brother resigned his membership in Washington's Metropolitan Club because that exclusive organization refused to have Negroes as members or as guests.

Bob is antagonistic toward Senator Karl Mundt because the South Dakota Republican conducted a continuous undercover campaign to undermine his work on the Rackets Committee while maintaining a façade of jovial friendship.

Mundt still is hostile toward Kennedy. Although he concedes that the Attorney General is "a very hard-driving worker" and has a "good knack for heading an investigative group," his personal regard for him is about as high as it would be for a rabid terrier.

"He had a lot of personality clashes on the committee," says Mundt. "He has an inability to work with people who might have a varying point of view— a lack of give and take. This is a bitter personal characteristic of Bob Kennedy's. He would not be successful serving in the legislature. His mental sullenness would kill him off rather quickly."

Senator Barry Goldwater, who also served on the Rackets Committee and whose political concepts run at an even broader angle to the Kennedys' views than do those of Mundt, does not share Mundt's assessment. Goldwater, who might be the Republican presidential or vice-presidential nominee against John Kennedy in 1964, likes Robert Kennedy personally and states: "I never was too worried about Bob."

The virile, white-haired Arizona lawmaker says: "He impressed me as a fellow who knew how long his rope was—how far he could go before he had to start looking for help. I'm quite impressed with the guy.

Any man who knows his own limitations is a fellow you can feel pretty safe with."

Robert Kennedy has crossed some powerful men—the bosses of America's biggest unions; the kings of the underworld and the thugs and goons who carry out their dirty work; powerful figures within both political parties; influential men of business and industry; and members of the United States Senate. If a man is to be known by the enemies he keeps, then Bob Kennedy is to be known by a strange and colorful assortment of foes. Not just Hoffa, the clever, loquacious Mundt, or Conger. But also individuals like Roy Cohn, a bright, ambitious, young New York lawyer who was a source of power and destruction in the life of Joe McCarthy; Senator Carl Curtis, a reactionary from the flatlands of Nebraska; Senator Homer Capehart, a homely Hoosier who has been a phenomenal success both at making money and winning elections; John Patterson, the vacillating Governor of Alabama who helped the Kennedys win the election in 1960 and became one of their most harassing problems in 1961; Senator Gordon Allott, a conscientious, hard-working Coloradan who sincerely seemed to believe that a man without courtroom experience should not be Attorney General; the late George Bender of Ohio who took over but obviously never filled the seat of Ohio's Senatorial giant, Robert A. Taft.

Robert Kennedy's friendships cut across an equally unusual range of men—Herbert C. Hoover, the indomitable symbol of American conservatism; William O. Douglas, the eloquent voice of American liberalism; Senator Joseph R. McCarthy, the pitiful demagogue from Wisconsin; Senator John McClellan, a monument of Southern responsibleness; Frank Sinatra, a controversial entertainer.

While it may be possible to categorize Robert Kennedy's friends with political labels, it is difficult to put the man himself in any particular slot. Shortly after he was elected President, John Kennedy was quoted in *Look* magazine as saying: "Bobby is caught in a cross current of labels we pin on people. We tend to check off an arbitrary list, add up the results and come up with a liberal or conservative. Bobby doesn't fit this. I could say that he is essentially conservative, but not on a matter like the minimum wage or a number of other issues. He acts pragmatically. I think he might once have been intolerant of liberals as such because his early experience was with that high-minded, high-speaking kind who never get anything done. That all changed the moment he met a liberal like Walter Reuther."

Ken O'Donnell recalls that Bob regarded himself as a Democrat when they were in Harvard immediately after World War II, although he was critical of some aspects of the Truman Administration and felt that Henry Wallace was "outrageous." But party affiliation in that period was as much a family matter as anything else for Robert Kennedy. Two grandfathers, John F. "Honey Fitz" Fitzgerald and Patrick J. Kennedy, were elected to public office as Democrats. His father, Joseph P. Kennedy, was an active party fund-raiser and officeholder during the first eight years of Franklin D. Roosevelt's administration. His brother, John, was elected to Congress as a Democrat.

"It was traditional in my family to be a Democrat," he says. "I identified myself with the Democratic party, but I did not feel nearly as strongly about it as I do now."

Robert Kennedy refuses to pinpoint himself as a liberal or a conservative. "I don't believe in labels," he explains. "They're somewhat phony." But he now is quite convinced that the Democratic party is his natural political home.

"As far as accomplishing something for the people, as far as motion is concerned, being activist, I just don't think there is any comparison between the two parties," says the Attorney General. "We would be stultified under the Republican party."

Robert Kennedy is as much at war with political lassitude as he is with mental, physical and moral softness. He is convinced that a nation reflects its people and that the American people themselves have shown a tendency toward flabbiness in recent years.

A fiercely competitive and even combative man, Kennedy believes humans must strive for excellence in all they do. He personally is constantly on the move in pursuit of this goal. He does not let a day pass without indulging in exercise to keep himself physically fit. He has developed a voracious appetite for reading —mostly history but some novels and suspense stories. He is possessed of high moral values, so much so that he sometimes is thought to be a puritan.

In the autumn, he follows closely the fortunes of the Baltimore Colts professional football team rather than the mediocre Washington Redskins and attends games whenever he can get away. He enjoys movies and stage musicals, but, as Ethel explains, "Bob never sees anything depressing." Although Ethel describes her husband as "a stoic about food," he does like steak and has a passion for anything with chocolate in or on it. He drinks only sparingly.

Since John and Robert Kennedy were reared in the same robust, stimulating atmosphere and have been inseparable associates in public life for many years, there naturally are many similarities between the two men. But there also are some very important differences.

Where John Kennedy can view almost any problem of state or humanity with dispassion and aloofness, Robert Kennedy invariably becomes emotionally involved in the job at hand and the people embroiled in it. Where John Kennedy's mind is a vast, intricate network that must probe and study and ponder before acting, Robert Kennedy's is a more simple, direct-current connection that moves automatically, decisively and instinctively. Where John Kennedy is a wholly self-possessed individual who abhors displays of emotion, Robert Kennedy is an intense human who can both rage and weep.

After fourteen years in House and Senate and one year in the Presidency, John Kennedy has made few personal enemies. Even the men who are in combat with him in the political arena—Richard Nixon, Barry Goldwater, Nelson Rockefeller, Illinois' flamboyant Senator Everett Dirksen and Indiana's rough little gut-fighter, Charlie Halleck—like John Kennedy personally. Robert Kennedy is far more adept than his brother at making enemies.

Joseph P. Kennedy, who has watched at close range the performances of Franklin D. Roosevelt, Winston Churchill, Herbert Hoover, Neville Chamberlain and James Michael Curley, once said with obvious parental pride that his son Jack was the "only perfect politician" he had ever known because Jack never alienated anyone. By the same standard, Robert Kennedy would be a most imperfect politician. But together the perfect politician and the imperfect politician have proved an unbeatable pair.

It never has bothered Robert Kennedy that he has been called the hatchet man for his brother. During the presidential campaign when politicians and party workers complained of brusque treatment from him, his reply was that he had a job to do and could not tolerate anything less than dedication and hard work from others in the campaign. "Let Jack be charming to them," he would add.

Robert Kennedy, then, is a man of paradoxes. He must be first, but invariably has been second. He despises hypocrisy, yet has an Irishman's love of politics —a profession that flourishes on hypocrisy. He can be rudely demanding of his employees, yet infuse them with absolute loyalty and devotion. He hates inefficiency, but is a bit disorganized himself. He can make friends and enemies with equal fervor. He is a puritan who enjoys associations among the worldly folk of Hollywood. He can run roughshod over others and then perform the most thoughtful and sentimental gestures for them. He is a determined spirit who always wins the game, often after being pushed into it by accident.

But of all the contradictions, none is quite so startling as the disparity between the personality and the physical appearance of Robert Kennedy. He is a man of magnificent temperament and impregnable will, the father of seven children and the most influential figure in President Kennedy's Administration. Yet he seems forever to resemble a bewildered sophomore about to embark upon his first date. The hangdog look was not invented by Robert Kennedy but it has been perfected by him. Preoccupied and a bit absent-minded, he moves from one achievement to the next with his head in a shy droop, his sandy hair rumpled and his eyes cast downward. His face, a light, masculine facsimile of Rose Kennedy's dark, birdlike beauty, is more that of a sensitive, pliable man than of a defiant conqueror. But there is one hint of the Goliath complex in it. When Robert Kennedy is particularly pleased, his face displays the amazed triumph of the canary that just swallowed the cat.

Chapter Four
The Middle Brother

LIKE ALL HIS BROTHERS AND SISTERS, ROBERT FRANCIS Kennedy was born in Massachusetts, that colorful political heterology where time and the immigration tide have forced the Lowells to speak to the Fitzgeralds and the Lodges to bow to the Kennedys. The date of his birth was November 20, 1925. The place was his parents' fashionable home on Naples Road in Brookline, a suburb of Boston.

The time was one of turmoil and excitement in the family. Joe Kennedy's financial wizardry already had made him a highly successful mystery man in Wall Street and he was about to begin a career as a producer and distributor of Hollywood-made motion pictures. By the time Robert, the seventh of the Kennedy children, was born, it was obvious that a dynamic money man like Joe Kennedy was too big for Boston. He had business interests in New York, Los Angeles, London and heaven knows where else. He also felt that his eldest daughters were approaching an age where they could be hurt by the anti-Irish, anti-Catholic snobbery of puritanical Boston.

Within a year after Robert's birth, Joe loaded his wife, seven children and a staff of servants aboard a private railroad car at a siding near Brookline and moved them in grand style to a new home in Riverdale, New York. This was the initial move of the nomadic Kennedys out of their native state. Yet always they would return to Massachusetts—to Boston to build their political fortunes; to Joe Kennedy's rambling white house at Hyannisport for leisurely summers and an annual Thanksgiving Day reunion. Robert Kennedy, who now owns a house beside those of his father and brother John in the big plot of ground on Nantucket Sound, says Hyannisport still is the place he regards as home.

The departure from Boston was most difficult for Rose Kennedy, a serene and lovely woman whose father, the colorful, diminutive John F. "Honey Fitz" Fitzgerald, had been the first Irish Catholic to be elected mayor of "The Hub." Although she obtained some of her education in New York and Europe, Rose was very much a part of the city which her father had presided over with a deft political hand, flowing oratory and repeated renditions of "Sweet Adeline." She was at home in the social, cultural and Catholic Church life in Boston. It also was in Boston in 1914 that she married Joseph P. Kennedy, the enterprising, popular son of Honey Fitz's long-time political ally, Patrick J. Kennedy.

Like Honey Fitz, Pat Kennedy had gravitated toward political office. He was elected six times to the Massachusetts Legislature, five times as a representative and once as a senator.

Even after Joe Kennedy moved his family to New York in 1926, Rose returned to a Boston hospital to give birth to Jean, in 1928, and to Edward, in 1932. She was attended by the same physician, Dr. Fred Good, who had been at her side through all her deliveries, starting with Joe, Jr., in 1915. Young Joe was born in Honey Fitz's summer home at Hull, a then-popular resort community at the end of an arm of land that reaches protectively around Hingham and Quincy Bays, about twenty miles southeast of Boston. John, Rosemary, Kathleen, Eunice, Patricia and Robert all were born between 1917 and 1925 in the homes occupied by Joe and Rose Kennedy in Brookline.

Robert Kennedy was born at the height of one of the most fabulous eras in American history. The nation, proud and cocky after winning its first big war fought on European soil, had made an almost complete break with its puritan past and was enjoying a complacency it probably never again would know. Prohibitionists thought they had dried the nation up with enactment of the 18th Amendment, but in reality they had made it wetter than ever before. And with a new twist—women drank and smoked right along with their menfolk for the first time. Women also had obtained the vote and two of them became state governors for the first time the year that Robert Kennedy was born. Science and Bible fundamentalists clashed in a Dayton, Tennessee, courtroom over the teaching of evolution. Millions of Japanese seethed with a sense of national humiliation because of a new United States immigration act barring them from a land made great by peoples who ventured to it from foreign shores. Isolationism was about to lose a battle on Capitol Hill over the Permanent Court of International Justice, and President Calvin Coolidge was fighting a limited war in Nicaragua without benefit of Congressional approval. Air travel was strengthening its embryo wings with first flights across oceans, around the North Pole and over the top of the globe.

When Robert was born, Joe, Jr., was ten and Jack was eight. Teddy came along seven years later. So, for much of his early life, Robert was the little brother in the middle of five sisters.

Years later, when Jack Kennedy was running in the 1960 presidential primary in Wisconsin, Robert Kennedy found himself caught in the shuffle between brothers. Teddy went into the state to campaign for

Jack and there made something of a headline splash by going off a high ski jump. "Everybody I met after that wanted to know first if I was Senator Kennedy, then if I was the fellow who went off the ski jump," says Robert. "Finally, they got me straight. I was the brother in the middle."

Of great concern to the elder Kennedys when Bobby was small was the fact that he was surrounded by sisters and might be weakened by their feminine influence. "My mother always said that was a terrible position to put any boy in," he says.

But the parents soon discovered that while Robert was "gentle and soft spoken in the house" he was tough and competitive in outdoor activity. He also was "unselfish and co-operative" with few, if any, worries on his mind, says his mother. Joe Kennedy, who takes great pride in the combative qualities of his offspring, has explained: "Bobby always had a lot of tenacity."

Both parents are convinced that Robert's personality was influenced by the gap of years dividing him from his older brothers and the fact he had a difficult time trying to keep apace of them. Joe and Rose Kennedy attempted to give him the same opportunities that Joe, Jr., and Jack had had. For instance, Rose Kennedy recalls her husband stating that Robert should get a trip to Latin America because Joe and Jack had been there. Among the four Kennedy boys, Robert was the smallest, the one with the poorest physical co-ordination and the one who, until he reached adulthood, showed the least interest in intellectual pursuits.

"Bobby never read as much as Joe or Jack before he went to college," said Joseph Kennedy in an interview before he suffered his paralyzing stroke in December 1961. "But now he is a prodigious reader."

Almost everyone who watched Robert Kennedy grow agrees that the amazing resolve he has exhibited in adult life was born of his attempts as a little boy to keep up with his older brothers.

His own earliest recollections are of exuberant family living during the summers at Hyannisport and during the winter months in a huge home in Bronxville, New York, to which the Kennedys moved about the time Teddy was born.

Among the four sisters who were older than he, the one closest to him was Eunice. Eunice had enough tomboy in her to be a rowdy playmate for her young brother. He still is in awe of her youthful abilities as a wrestler, recalling that "she was terrific" in combat with him and one of his boy friends.

Once Eunice tossed a handful of chocolate frosting across the dinner table at her unsuspecting brother. He immediately began chasing her around the room. After he cornered her, he put his head down and charged at her like a bull. But Eunice was a more adept matador than he was a bull. She stepped aside and he drove his tousled head into a table, cutting a bloody gash in it.

"I dropped everything. I always fell down. I always bumped my nose or my head," he says, looking back at his awkward childhood.

In the tool shed of the Bronxville home, he pulled a radiator over on his foot and broke a toe. At a formal party in the same home, he grabbed up a glass of tomato juice with such force that its crimson contents shot upward, splattering the ceiling, the table linen and the elegant clothing of his parents' guests. He also got tar in his eyes once and spent three worrisome days before it was determined his sight would not be affected.

Despite clumsy mishaps, he is remembered by visitors to the Kennedy home as a polite and delightful youngster. T. J. (Ted) Reardon, Jack Kennedy's administrative assistant in the House, the Senate and most recently in the White House, first went to Hyannisport when he was Joe's roommate at Harvard in the middle thirties. He recalls Robert as a friendly, slightly shy and well-mannered little boy.

K. LeMoyne Billings first met him about the same time, when he went to Palm Beach with Jack, then his roommate at Choate School. Lem's recollection is this: "Bobby was a hell of a nice little boy, one of the nicest I ever met. He always was responsible, friendly and thoughtful."

In his earliest years, the idol of Robert Kennedy's life was Joe, Jr., rather than Jack. With their father away frequently on business, the smaller children—Eunice, Pat, Bobby, Jean and Teddy—depended heavily on Joe, Jr., for leadership, especially in outdoor sports. Jack, who was two years younger and less extroverted than Joe, was not as dominant a figure in their lives.

"My brother Joe took the greatest interest in us," says Robert Kennedy. "He taught us to sail, to swim, to play football and baseball. After he was killed, Jack assumed a greater interest in all of us."

Because Rosemary, the oldest of the Kennedy girls, was forced by frail health to lead a less active life than her brothers and sisters, Kathleen was the sister who set the pace for the younger children.

"Joe and Kathleen were a great influence upon the younger children," says Rose Kennedy. "They were beloved and looked up to by the rest of the family. Joe was intelligent, a superb athlete and taught the younger children to swim and boat and play ball. Kathleen was gay and well read and knowledgeable about many things, including politics. She was inspiring to the younger members of the family. The older children would take over the younger ones as we got older. They would compete in sports with them at home or at St. Moritz."

Joe was very much like his father, a brawny, handsome, gregarious, demanding youth, who made the smaller children toe the mark during the many absences of their father. Between Joe, Jr., and Jack, competition always was keen and often belligerent. Robert recalls hiding upstairs with his sisters at Hyannisport while Joe and Jack fought furiously on the first floor.

Joseph P. Kennedy, convinced that rivalry between his two oldest boys would strengthen the character of each, intervened only when they became too rough. But Rose Kennedy attempted to limit disputes among her children and between parents and offspring. She believed that family quarrels could be curtailed by eliminating as many sources of potential conflict as possible. She noted that disputes arose quickly in a large family in a corridor leading to a single bathroom. Additional bathrooms meant less conflict so she got a house with many bathrooms.

"We always discussed the situations, if possible, before they happened," says Mrs. Kennedy. "With the little children, for instance, we would say, 'You will get your candy after lunch, after you eat your vegetables and meat so you can get strong and so you can play ball like your brothers and your father.' "

Although the brothers and sisters were permitted wide latitude in their activities as a means of making them responsible citizens, there were certain rules they had to follow.

"They could go sailing," says Rose Kennedy. "But they always had to tell the governess which direction they were going. In case of fog we would know where to find them. They all had to take turns at the tennis court and stick to a schedule that was fair to everybody. We wanted to make everybody understand that everybody is going to have a turn. All the children had to understand also that they must be considerate of the staff and go to the village when the chauffeur would go on errands and not just make him drive in on a trip."

Meals were served at a specific time and the children were required to assemble five minutes before the deadline. Rose Kennedy believes that mealtimes provide a period for instructing growing children that often is lost in purposeless small talk. The elder Kennedys shared even their formal dinners with their growing children, including a state banquet they gave for King George VI and his Queen Elizabeth when Joe was Ambassador to England.

Rose Kennedy found it impossible to remember all the vital statistics about nine children. "Out of desperation," she explains, "I went to a neighborhood bookstore one day and bought a card file." In this file she recorded the various ailments her youngsters suffered and other data. The file shows that Robert suffered no major illness or accident that caused great alarm in the family.

When he was ten years old, however, he did come down with pneumonia and was whisked to a Boston hospital at the height of the summer swimming and boating season on Cape Cod. Patricia was in the same hospital at the same time with an appendectomy and one of her nurses was a young woman named Luella Hennessey.

When Joe and Rose Kennedy visited the two ailing children in the hospital, they told them they could choose one of the nurses to go home with them during their convalescence. Miss Hennessey, in a 1960 magazine article, recalled that while she was not aware of this, she did notice that Pat frequently sent her to Robert's room on what seemed to be concocted errands. She was their choice and went to Hyannisport to care for both children. After that, Miss Hennessey traveled much with the Kennedys and has cared for all but one of the grandchildren of Rose and Joe Kennedy at birth.

The elder Kennedys do not recall that Robert, as a youngster, displayed a special aptitude for any career. One family friend does believe, however, that of all the Kennedy children, he is the one best equipped by personality and determination to have gone out and made a fortune of his own had Joseph P. Kennedy not made it for him. A delightful little tale of enterprise from his boyhood casts some doubt on this, however.

Like all the Kennedy youngsters, he had only a modest allowance when he was growing up. While living in Bronxville, he decided to supplement this income by selling *The Saturday Evening Post* and *The Ladies' Home Journal* to his neighbors. At the time he had a pet pig named Porky and the two of them—determined little boy and waddling little pig—made the rounds on foot selling the *Post* and the *Journal*. Later, neighbors noted that the boy was riding a bicycle and the pig was wandering along behind. Finally, just before he abandoned his career as a magazine salesman, the same neighbors saw him riding his route in the back of the family's chauffeur-driven Rolls Royce. The escapade in enterprise ended with Dave, the chauffeur, delivering the magazines by himself and with many unsold issues stacked in the boy's room.

Porky still holds an especially warm place in Robert Kennedy's heart. When he was thirty-two and at the height of the Rackets Committee probe, the committee staff presented him with a second pig. The gift immediately brought the long-departed Porky to his mind. With mock tragedy in his voice, he said that any frustrations he has suffered as an adult are due to losing Porky as a child.

He was more successful with another boyhood foray

into the business world. He decided there was profit in raising and selling rabbits—"just plain white rabbits, the kind that have a lot of babies." So he set up a hutch in the tool shed and made $42 at this enterprise. Rose Kennedy placed the money in an account in a Hyannis bank, and it is still there.

When he was older, Robert, like Joe, Jr., and Jack, worked briefly at the Columbia Trust Company, a Boston bank which Joseph P. Kennedy owned. He enjoyed the work and was impressed especially by one particular duty—that of collecting rents from poverty-hounded residents in East Boston tenement houses. Never before had he seen huge families crowded into tiny, stifling flats or people sleeping on fire escapes.

The only difficulty Rose Kennedy remembers having with him when he was growing up was over his casual approach to clothing. She says: "Bobby never had much concern about his clothes. He would appear on dress-up occasions wearing a coat of one color and trousers of another."

Mrs. Kennedy, a devout Catholic, started with her first-born, Joe, Jr., to give personal religious instruction to all her children. This spiritual training appears to have left an especial imprint upon Robert Kennedy, who believes his opposition toward racial and religious discrimination has its roots in "my upbringing in religion."

"I try to have tolerance toward viewpoints, tolerance toward ideas," says the Attorney General.

The elder Kennedys never attempted to segregate their children from other youngsters for reasons of racial, religious or financial background. In fact, among the eight or ten regular playmates Bobby had at Hyannisport when he was small were two Negro boys, sons of a laundress who lived about three blocks from the Kennedy house.

In her religious instruction, Mrs. Kennedy always sought to impress upon her children the significance of the blessed sacrament and of Good Friday, Easter Sunday, Christmas and other events important to Catholics.

She recalls: "We always impressed upon them the importance of stopping at church when going by and not just waiting until Sunday. We would tell them why we make the way of the Cross and there would be many references to the Holy Land. The older children had been there and all went eventually. We also stressed the necessity of frequent communion by all members of the household and of observing the feasts of the saints for which they were named, St. Joseph, St. John, and so on."

Of her third son, Rose Kennedy says: "Bobby has been a great joy and blessing to me and my husband always. He has taken his religion seriously and still does. We never had any worries about him."

When Joseph P. Kennedy was home from his roamings about the world and the jobs he performed for Franklin D. Roosevelt, he of course was the dominant figure in the household. He led his children in stimulating conversation at the dinner table and supervised their acquisition of skill on the playing field. Above all, he demanded that they know what was happening in the world and that they always play to win.

Much has been written about this remarkable man who long ago decided that one of his sons would be President of the United States and lived to see his dream fulfilled. Much more has been written about his amazing offspring. Yet Joe Kennedy maintained he and his wife possessed no magic formula that turned their children into unusual adults. "If I knew the secret, I'd tell you," said Kennedy, "because I think it ought to be written."

Certainly one thing Joe Kennedy did for his children was to make each financially secure with a gift of one million dollars on his or her twenty-first birthday. In this way, Kennedy made it possible for them to exert to the fullest the spirit of determination and independence they had acquired from him.

Although Robert Kennedy was just four when the crash of 1929 began spreading its tentacles through the economy of the nation, he felt none of the effects that millions of starving and homeless children would in the next decade.

His education began in the public and private schools in Riverdale, continued through public and private schools in Bronxville, and then shifted to the elite Gibbs School in London when his father went there as Ambassador to the Court of St. James in 1937. Upon his return to America when war broke out, Robert Kennedy was enrolled in St. Paul's, a preparatory school in Concord, N. H., but his stay there was short. As soon as Rose Kennedy learned that St. Paul's was an Episcopal rather than a Catholic school, she withdrew him and sent him to Portsmouth Priory, a school run by the Benedictines in Rhode Island. After three years at Portsmouth Priory, he went to Milton Academy in Massachusetts for his last year of high school.

Looking back at his years as a migratory student, Kennedy remarks: "I went to ten or twelve schools, I think."

In none of them did he make much impression as a serious student. He distinguished himself primarily on the playing fields rather than in the classrooms. Unlike his two older brothers, who were good students, he devoted his energies and scrappy spirit almost solely to outdoor activities.

He forced himself to excel at football, baseball, sailing, swimming, tennis, and during the family's stay in

Great Britain, at cricket and soccer. He was a hard-hiking Cub Scout in New York and an enthusiastic Boy Scout in England. He did not join the Boy Scouts in London, however, until they revised their oath so that members did not have to swear allegiance to the King.

At a time when he was in the formative years of his life, the major discussion at the family dinner table and in the family living room concerned the steps Franklin D. Roosevelt was taking toward involvement of America in the war with Hitler. Joe, Jr., and Jack discussed the issue vehemently with their father who was deeply opposed to involvement. Robert tried to enter the conversations, but friends recall that he had more difficulty making himself heard and listened to than the older boys.

Robert Kennedy recalls the eerie feeling he got when, on a tour of the European continent with his parents, he saw long lines of militant goose-stepping Nazi soldiers. He also remembers the somber moment when he and his family heard Neville Chamberlain, on September 3, 1939, declare war on Germany and Italy.

He reflected his father's views that America could and should stay out of the war, but at thirteen or fourteen there was little he could do about it. Joe, Jr., so strongly shared Joe, Sr.'s, disenchantment with FDR and the "interventionists" that he went to the Democratic national convention in 1940 as a Massachusetts delegate pledged to Postmaster General James A. Farley for the presidential nomination, although everyone knew Roosevelt would be renominated for a third term. Even Jack, with his usual unemotional detachment, agreed with some of his father's arguments in *Why England Slept,* the best-seller he originally wrote at Harvard in 1939-40.

Robert Kennedy's only outlet for his partisanship seemed to be to get into fist fights with his British schoolmates over which country—the United States or England—really won World War I.

Like the rest of his family he shied away from drinking and smoking during his school years, and collected $2,000 from his father when he was twenty-one for avoiding these indulgences.

At Milton Academy there was some resentment among other students that the Ambassador's son would not join in their frivolity. But it was short-lived. Robert became popular as he proved his prowess in sports and joined his fellow students in other non-alcoholic, non-nicotine school activities. He even made a try at the glee club with his high voice and broad "a."

Whether he learned much at Milton is questionable. But he did make a friendship there that still is the closest he has outside his family. It is with David Hackett, who recalls that while Kennedy was not the best natural athlete at Milton, he "made up for it in other ways." The other ways were perseverance and toughness.

When Robert Kennedy was appointed Attorney General, one of his first acts was to name Hackett as one of his assistants.

At the time Bob was graduated from Milton Academy in 1943, the United States was deeply involved in the great war that the Kennedys thought America should not enter. Joe, Jr., was a Navy pilot about to depart for England. Jack was a PT boat commander in the South Pacific. Young Joe urged Robert to follow his course and join the Naval Air Corps as soon as he was eighteen years old, which was November 20, 1943. He accepted the advice, signed for the V-5 program and was sent to Bates College in Maine for eight months' training.

This was a time of heroism for most American boys

and especially for the vigorous Kennedys. In the months just before Robert entered the Navy, Jack lived through a harrowing experience in the Solomon Islands that marked him for life as an individual of great courage and physical stamina. After his PT boat was ripped in half by a Japanese destroyer in Blackett Strait on the black tropical night of August 2, 1943, he guided his crew from island to island looking for rescuers. Jack himself suffered a painful back injury, but despite his own pain, he swam for hours in enemy waters, towing an injured crewman behind him on a life belt. And later performed the same feat for additional hours. Finally, due to Jack Kennedy's unyielding efforts, the crew was rescued.

However, the epoch of World War II carrying the greatest emotional impact for the Kennedys came almost a year later, in July, 1944.

By that time young Joe had flown so many missions from his naval air base in England that he was scheduled to return to the United States. Instead, he volunteered for an extremely perilous experiment with a potential for saving human life commensurate with the risk.

Midway through 1944, as the European phase of the conflict seemed to be going in favor of the Allies, the Nazis began a new type of assault by air upon London, using V-2 rockets.

Unlike Adolf Hitler's V-1 buzz bombs which traveled only about 300 miles an hour, this new *wunderwaffen* went about 3,000 miles an hour. Planes could not catch it nor could any weapon then available to the Allies shoot it down, as had been done eight out of ten times with the V-1. The new rockets hit before their victims knew they were coming. Their launching sites seemed immune from bombs dropped by airplanes. The conquest of the world swung within reach of Hitler and no plan for combating the V-2 was too desperate to attempt.

The plan for which Joe Kennedy volunteered called for a PBY-4 Liberator, heavily loaded with explosives, to be flown over the English Channel, then set on course by the pilot who would parachute to safety. The theory was that the bomber would be guided by radio to the V-2 launching pad. But before Joe and his co-pilot could parachute from the Liberator, it exploded and both were killed.

Nineteen-year-old Robert Kennedy undoubtedly had visions of being a war hero like his two older brothers. But the Navy did not co-operate. After eight months at Bates, he was transferred to the V-12 naval officer training program and sent to Bowdoin College and then to Harvard, where he was put in the ROTC.

Restless and bored, he resorted to exactly the same course Jack had followed early in the war when he got Washington to change his orders and send him into the combat-ripped South Pacific rather than the peaceful Panama Canal area. Robert went to see Navy Secretary James Forrestal, who had helped Jack get into the heart of the fighting war. Forrestal, an old Wall Street friend of Joseph P. Kennedy, was instrumental in having Robert transferred from Harvard to the newly commissioned destroyer named after his dead brother, the *Joseph P. Kennedy, Jr.*

Then the war ended and the subsequent months of Robert Kennedy's life read like pages out of *Mr. Roberts.* They were spent in tedious paint-chipping and radar-watching in the Caribbean with not an enemy in sight.

When he got out of the Navy early in 1946, he plunged into political combat for the first time, helping Jack in the savage Democratic primary fight to determine who would succeed James Michael Curley as Congressman from Boston's 11th District.

With Jack nominated in a district that never has elected a Republican, Robert Kennedy left on a two-month trip to Latin America with Lem Billings.

Billings recalls that Robert's reactions on the journey through Latin America were basically the same as Jack's when he and Lem had made a tour through Europe in 1937 on the eve of World War II. "Bob had the same inquisitive mind," says Billings. "It was obvious to us then that Latin America was ripe for Communism and we talked a great deal about it."

Both were astounded at the economic plight of a Brazilian they met who was the foreman in charge of constructing one of the fanciest tourist hotels on Copacabana Beach. They went one day to the home of the foreman and discovered that this highly skilled man, who in the United States would draw a substantial salary, was living in a tin shack on a hillside. They realized then there was no middle class in Latin America and that one day changes would have to be made in the economy of the entire area.

Billings says Robert also was "extremely interested" in the situation in Argentina where dictator Juan Perón still ruled with his wife Eva as a full partner. This interest was heightened by the fact that their plane was not permitted to land in Buenos Aires. They had to set down in Uruguay and make their way into Argentina by land.

Robert Kennedy returned to Harvard in the fall of 1946. This was a time of hope and of revolt in a nation that had just won the biggest war in history and was ready to lead the world in what Americans expected to be a long period of peace and prosperity. The veteran, back from Normandy and Guadalcanal and Anzio and Lingayen Gulf, was ready to bring new order and new vigor to the nation. Everywhere across the land that autumn, old political faces were rejected for new ones. Jack Kennedy was one of the new faces. In Southern California, a bright young naval veteran named Richard Nixon defeated long-secure New Deal Congressman Jerry Voorhis. Henry Cabot Lodge returned from the war to unseat one of the most colorful and successful figures in Massachusetts politics, Senator David I. Walsh. Joe McCarthy, a rugged ex-Marine, ended the brilliant La Follette dynasty in Wisconsin.

Robert Kennedy, however, showed no particular qualities of leadership at Harvard during this period, although as usual he met every test on the football field. "I didn't go to class very much," he says. "I used to talk and argue a lot, mostly about sports and politics. I began thinking about issues about the time I went to college."

Ken O'Donnell, his inseparable pal around the haunts of Cambridge, says: "Bob was about like I was. He got good marks with a minimum of effort. Of course he always was interested in history and politics."

Robert Kennedy, Ken O'Donnell and a tightly knit group of cronies—most of them football players—spent many hours discussing the problems of the nation and the world in that era, 1946-48, just as college students did everywhere in America. "We were the dozen most know-it-alls in the history of the world," recalls O'Donnell.

"At home we always discussed issues and sports," says Robert Kennedy. "Because of that I had more knowledge than the other students. But in some areas I had no knowledge, and no particular feeling about certain issues. I was for the veterans housing bill right after the war, but I know more about issues today and feel much more strongly."

O'Donnell's portrait of Robert Kennedy at Harvard

is: "In college in those years most of the guys were older than Bob and he was less sure of himself. He was not a dominant factor in the group. Bob didn't go to social affairs or dances. He went with the common herd. His friends were persons who couldn't scrape twenty-five cents together. Bob was like the rest of us—finding himself."

Like his brothers before him, Robert Kennedy became a member of Hasty Pudding, Spee Club and Varsity Club at Harvard, but his happiest times were those spent with his football buddies. On a couple of occasions he dragged some of the gridiron gang along with him to social events open to the son of the former Ambassador to the Court of St. James and not to offspring of lesser-known families. But the experiment proved a dismal failure. Robert Kennedy's attitude about very social events still is: "Nobody who goes to those things all the time makes any real contribution."

After graduation from Harvard in 1948, he was sent by the *Boston Post,* which practically was a journalistic adjunct of the Kennedy family in those days, to the Middle East to write about the war between the Arabs and the Jews.

In that troubled area, he had a mysterious experience. He had intended to ride from Tel Aviv to Jerusalem by convoy, until he met a tank captain who had been a friend of his sister, Kathleen.

Kathleen, like young Joe, had been a formative influence upon Robert and her other younger siblings. Like Joe also, she died in a plane crash earlier that same year, 1948.

The tank captain suggested to Kennedy that he ride with him to Jerusalem and he accepted. The tank came through safely. The convoy was destroyed by Arab raiders.

Robert Kennedy also demonstrated on that journalistic adventure some of the insight that later proved so successful in domestic politics. Although the Arabs far outnumbered the Jews, he felt the Jews would win the war because they "had much more spirit and zest and determination and discipline. They were tougher inwardly and outwardly than the Arabs."

These basically are the same reasons why the team of Robert and Jack Kennedy was able to trounce all competitors for the Democratic presidential nomination in 1960 and then go on to defeat Richard Nixon in the bid for the big prize.

After leaving the Middle East, Robert Kennedy went to Germany to watch the Berlin airlift operation. He also attempted to enter communist Hungary but was refused admission by the Communists who charged he was a Catholic spy who had been sent by New York's Francis Cardinal Spellman to see imprisoned Joseph Cardinal Mindszenty.

He enrolled in the University of Virginia law school when he returned to the United States and there accomplished a feat of which he still is extremely proud. As head of the student forum, he invited a number of outstanding Americans to speak on the campus at Charlottesville. Among them was his father, who used the forum to urge that America make itself an impregnable "arsenal of democracy" and not tie itself to military defense of western Europe; and his brother, Representative John F. Kennedy, who criticized foreign policy mistakes in western Europe and Indo-China but favored strong military and diplomatic alliances among the nations of the free world. Other speakers included former New Deal trust-buster Thurmond Arnold, *New York Times* columnist Arthur Krock, Associate Supreme Court Justice William O. Douglas, Senator Joseph R. McCarthy, and the distinguished American Negro diplomat, Ralph Bunche. There was considerable opposition to Bunche's appearance because a Negro never had been permitted to make a speech at the then segregated southern university. But Kennedy stuck by his beliefs, and Bunche made the speech. The Attorney General still cites this as one of the accomplishments of which he is most proud.

As a result of Justice Douglas's visit to the University of Virginia in that winter of 1950-51, Robert Kennedy went on a fascinating adventure five years later. The Justice, an old friend of Joe Kennedy, and one of the best traveled men in the world, discussed some of his past journeys with Robert and said he planned to make a trip into Soviet-controlled Central Asia. He asked Bob to go along.

Douglas tried unsuccessfully for four years to get a visa. Finally in 1955, he and Robert made a six-week swing through five Central Asian Republics of the Soviet Union. Some of the areas they toured had not had an outside visitor since the Russian Revolution. The trip was an awakener for Kennedy. He and Douglas were detoured into Siberia by the Communists so they would not see the huge slave labor camps at Karaganda, a city in Kazakhstan. They found wherever they went that men in military uniform were doing manual labor—laying bricks and pipes, putting up buildings, tending the oil fields.

They were not permitted to take their own interpreter but were furnished one by the Russians. Kennedy was impressed that people found their way into churches and that there even was something of a religious revival in progress despite the Communists' constant campaign against religion. He also discovered that Soviet Labor unions concerned themselves only with sanitary conditions in factories and had no control over wages, which were set by the state. He said upon his return he could not understand the affinity of some American liberals for the communist system because it was diametrically opposed to liberal principles.

At the end of a long interview with *U. S. News and World Report* in October, 1955, he was asked if he would like to go to Russia again. He replied: "I had enough of it."

"Would you like to live there?" asked the magazine editors.

"No. I am a firm believer in the capitalistic system," said Kennedy.

The editors put their final question: "Do you think with all our troubles and all our friction and all our defects, we may be better off than they are?"

"I think anybody who doesn't think so should take a trip there," said Kennedy. "I am hopeful, like everybody in the world, that what happened at the Geneva conference and what will happen at the meetings of the foreign ministers will mean peace for us all. However, on the basis of what I saw and learned in Russia, I am very distrustful that we will get anything other than smiles.

"We are dealing with a government to whom God, the family or the individual means nothing, and whose practice it has been in the past to make promises and treaties to serve their purposes and to break them when it has been to their advantage. It can only be suicidal for us during this period, on the basis of smiles, to strengthen Russia and weaken ourselves."

At the time he spoke those prophetic words, Robert Kennedy did not know that within six years he would be sitting as chief adviser and confidant to the President of the United States during a period when America and the Soviet Union trembled on the brink of nuclear war.

When Douglas first suggested the trip to the Soviet Union, Robert Kennedy was in his last year at the University of Virginia. He was graduated in mid-1951. He briefly considered going into private law practice in New York, but instead became a lawyer in the agency of government he one day would head—the Department of Justice.

Chapter Five
Mistress of
Hickory Hill

NINE MONTHS AFTER HE BECAME ATTORNEY GENERAL, Robert F. Kennedy was asked what he considered the major achievement of his life. He was at the moment nibbling a piece of toast and sipping a glass of milk before rushing to the White House to witness President Kennedy's signing of three laws that would arm the Attorney General with broad new interstate authority to fight gambling, narcotics traffic and other crimes. Ethel Kennedy sat across an oval mahogany table from her husband and three of the little Kennedys romped through the gracious dining room at Hickory Hill.

When the question was asked by a breakfast guest, the Attorney General dropped his head, fixed his eyes on the worn oak flooring and pondered fifty, possibly sixty seconds. His slow and almost somber deliberation prompted Ethel to shoot a blithe verbal dart across the table. "That quick mind!" she quipped.

The Attorney General pondered on, recalling the senatorial and presidential elections he helped his brother to win, the success he had had in spotlighting corruption in the union movement, the writing of his book, *The Enemy Within,* his handling of difficult problems at the Department of Justice. Then abruptly he was transformed into a happy leprechaun. His face lit up and wrinkled up at the same moment, like that of a child who has for the first time seen and touched a newborn puppy. He flashed a smile across the table at his wife and, in a voice filled with playful mockery, declared triumphantly: "Marrying Ethel."

Ethel Kennedy accepted the tribute in the manner in which it was paid—with laughter—and responded: "It certainly took you long enough to decide."

This bit of frivolity ended and Robert Kennedy went on to discuss seriously the accomplishments he found most satisfying. They, of course, were in the public arena, but there was more than jest in the Attorney General's claim that "marrying Ethel" was his greatest achievement. For, as his friend, *Time* magazine correspondent Hugh Sidey, points out, "even Bobby Kennedy's most adamant critics admit that his home life is delightful."

The same verdict is expressed by Jacques Lowe, a New York photographer who has been taking Kennedy family portraits since 1957 and who was in the earliest days of the New Frontier dubbed "the court photographer" by White House correspondents. After finishing a picture layout for the Catholic magazine *Sign* in the summer of 1961, Lowe said the Robert Kennedys and their seven youngsters are "the happiest family I have ever met."

The two oldest children, Kathleen Hartington, born in 1951, and Joseph Patrick, who arrived a year later, were named for the Attorney General's sister and brother, who were killed in airplane crashes. The five younger children were born between 1954 and 1959.

They are Robert Francis, Jr., David Anthony, Mary Courtney, Michael LeMoyne, and Mary Kerry.

With nine Kennedys and an assortment of hired help living under a single roof, no one person can take full credit for the jolly and robust atmosphere that prevails at Hickory Hill, a three-story, white Georgian mansion that stands on a knoll in McLean, Virginia. Yet as mistress of this happy bedlam, Ethel Kennedy is the most constant influence in the lives of her children, just as her mother-in-law, Mrs. Joseph P. Kennedy, was with her brood of nine youngsters. Ethel is a slim, vivacious woman with brown eyes and sun-bleached hair, who looks more like a singles champion at Wimbledon than the wife of a Cabinet officer and mistress of an historic estate.

Similarities between the Attorney General's wife and his mother are remarkable. Ethel is as much a Kennedy in spirit and energy as any of Rose Fitzgerald's daughters. In her flair for fashion and grooming and her dedication to a huge family, Ethel is even more like Rose Kennedy than some of the Kennedy girls. No less an authority than Joseph P. Kennedy himself has proudly proclaimed that Ethel "acts like a Kennedy."

Nineteen-year-old Robert Kennedy may have been captivated by these resemblances to the women of his own clan when he first met seventeen-year-old Ethel Skakel of Greenwich, Connecticut, in 1944 at a ski lodge at Mont Tremblant, Quebec, Canada. Jean Kennedy, Ethel's roommate at Manhattanville College of the Sacred Heart which at that time was in New York City, had interested her brothers, Robert and Edward, and her sisters, Eunice and Pat, in joining the Skakel family for a Christmas holiday skiing party.

Ethel recalls her meeting with Bob Kennedy in this way: "He was momentarily mad about me. He took me out for two weeks. Then he started taking out my sister Pat. She is three years older than I am—and much prettier and more intellectual."

Robert Kennedy and Ethel Skakel met at an exciting instant in world history, and one that was not conducive to courtship. Allied armored divisions were thundering in on Nazi Germany from east and west. United States forces had just secured the Philippines. And Robert Kennedy, eager to be in the fighting as his two older brothers had been, was beginning the Navy's V-12 officer training program.

Ethel and Robert had occasional dates during the five and a half years between their first meeting and the beginning of an intensive six-month courtship that preceded their 1950 wedding. They were married in Greenwich, with John F. Kennedy as best man.

The dates they had over the five and a half years frequently were for school events at the College of the Sacred Heart, which Ethel entered after graduating from Manhattanville, or at Harvard and the University of Virginia where Bob studied. In 1946, Ethel, who had been reared in a Republican family, joined Robert in helping elect John Kennedy to the House of Representatives from the 11th District of Massachusetts. Asked by a reporter whether her father objected to her romantic interest in a Democrat, Ethel replied: "Yes, but in a humorous vein."

The telephone, which has taken a major role in keeping the Kennedy clan united despite their individual travels, also was utilized frequently by Robert in his courtship of Ethel. Ethel doubts that her early interest in politics was an asset to romance, and when asked whether their mutual liking for campaigns and elections has since contributed to marital togetherness, she responds with an emphatic "no."

Of the seven attractive young men and women who have married the children of Joseph P. Kennedy, Ethel was the best equipped by family background, training and personal taste to integrate immediately into their way of life. She was the product of a big New England Catholic family. She excelled in sports and loved outdoor activities. She was both competitive and gay by nature. She also had been exposed to the Kennedys for six years before she married into the family and had acquired an enthusiastic admiration for them.

"Ethel had no difficulty blending into the Kennedy family, not one problem," says a close personal friend. "She loves all their noise and rowdyism and excitement."

Her devotion to her husband's family also apparently has helped Ethel through the difficult time when her own parents were killed in an airplane crash in 1955.

Other in-laws have found it less easy to merge themselves into the stimulating self-centered world of the Kennedys. To do so requires a young husband or wife occasionally to sit outside an exclusive little domain; to bob up smiling when pushed into a swimming pool; to devote talents and energy to the family's dominant cause: the political achievements of Joe Kennedy's sons.

Peter Lawford, a debonair British-born actor who attained modest success in motion pictures on his own, found the going tough in the early years of his marriage to rangy, dark-haired Patricia Kennedy. His difficulties were compounded by the fact that Joe Kennedy, who had been an intimate of the gaudy Hollywood scene as an executive of Pathé and Keith-Albee-Orpheum companies and the producer of Gloria Swanson pictures in the late twenties, made clear his distaste for the idea of an actor as a son-in-law. Despite this black beginning, friends report Lawford and the Kennedys have adjusted to each other rather well in recent years.

Jacqueline Kennedy, the President's wife, has held herself aloof from some of the rigorous demands of her husband's family. She decided long ago to fight for the preservation of her own individuality, which rates the cloistered worlds of art and the fox hunt ahead of those of touch football and bare-knuckle politics. The Kennedys generally admire her independence.

Although Ethel and Jacqueline Kennedy are dissimilar—the former being gregarious and animated, the latter introspective and reserved—they share a warm affection for each other.

Jacqueline never has given a public assessment of Ethel's skill as a touch football player, but Jack Kennedy stated his verdict a few years ago. He said: "Ethel's really good. You ought to see her run and pass."

"Touch football games with the Kennedys are mostly all very much the same," Ethel explains. "Everyone wants to cover Pat, be on Bobby's team, avoid Eunice and watch the guests go out for a pass up against the house."

Like Jacqueline, Ethel Kennedy is an adept horsewoman and in her girlhood cleared a hurdle at six feet, nine inches.

Prior to their marriage, Robert Kennedy did not ride horseback and even scoffed at Ethel's love of the sport. Under her tutelage, however, he learned and the two now gallop across the Virginia hills for exercise.

If there is a secret to the success of Ethel Kennedy's marriage, it probably is that she attempts to keep up with her active husband in any endeavor he undertakes. When it's touch football on the snow-covered east lawn at Hickory Hill, Ethel is there, plunging through scrimmage, darting out to tag the ball carrier or to snag a pass. When her husband goes out for his morning swim in the summer, or for tennis, Ethel joins him.

"I play to win," says Ethel. "I certainly don't let him win. But he usually does." With wifely pride, she adds: "Every day, I'm more amazed at his stamina."

A newswoman asked Ethel recently to name her favorite sport. "Whatever we happen to be playing at the time," was her immediate and revealing answer.

Ethel was a daily spectator during the three years that Robert Kennedy and the Senate Rackets Committee laid bare before a nationwide television audience the thievery and thuggery of hoodlum labor chieftains and their accomplices in the offices of management. She vacated her front-row seat briefly in 1958 to give birth to her sixth child, Michael LeMoyne, but was back again a few weeks later.

When Robert Kennedy has marched into political battle for his brother Jack, Ethel Kennedy has gone along to do whatever chore is assigned her. "In the 1946 campaign, my main contribution was licking the flaps of envelopes," she remembers.

In 1952, when Jack pulled off his spectacular defeat of Senator Henry Cabot Lodge, it was ringing doorbells, chatting with housewives and participating in teas. By the 1960 presidential election, Ethel was a full-fledged political campaigner. She barnstormed the country, speaking on behalf of her brother-in-law, shaking hands and making votes. "I die every time I have to speak," she confides, "but I love politics."

She has one highly prized testimonial to her skill on the campaign trail. James Michener, that superb chronicler of life and love in the South Pacific, watched her in action in the autumn of 1960. Later he wrote that Ethel "is one of the most politically sophisticated women I have ever known."

Robert and Ethel Kennedy scored a dual triumph when on a diplomatic mission they invaded Africa in the summer of 1961 like a couple of friendly social workers, exhibiting deep concern for the well-being of the people they met. The occasion was the Ivory Coast Republic's celebration of its first year of independence from France. President Kennedy considered the event important enough to send his brother as his personal emissary.

Life magazine's talented maverick, Anne Chamberlin, accompanied the Kennedys on their colorful swing through the little African nation and reported that "Ethel Kennedy's charm turned out to be a secret weapon of major dimensions."

The trip occurred just two months after Jacqueline Kennedy had proved the sensation of Western Europe when she and her husband visited Paris, Vienna and London.

After paying tribute to Robert Kennedy's "magic" among the natives of the Ivory Coast Republic, *Life* said: "Abetting him throughout was a heretofore little-known Kennedy, his lively wife Ethel, who beguiled the Ivory Coast as her sister-in-law Jacqueline Kennedy had bewitched Paris. Off on a jaunt with Bob to visit villages, she heard the prefect had ten children. Ethel, mother of seven, unseated previous local views of Americans by remarking, 'I'm jealous.' Both she and Bob spoke careful school book French during their three-day stay and did well enough to provoke a local linguist to say: 'She speaks excellent French and he defends himself.' "

Ethel had approached the official assignment with serious dedication. "Traveling in an official capacity as we were, more attention was focused upon us," she said in explaining her feeling about the trip. "I think this is especially true at this time with the birth of new nations in Africa. Of course, the prime responsibility was on my husband's shoulders."

Ethel purchased some French language records and with their aid studied in advance of the Ivory Coast trip, and also read several books and articles on the new republic's background. She has continued to study French with the expectation that she and the Attorney General may have other presidential assignments as a husband-wife emissary team.

Their next travel assignment required not only French, but Japanese and German. During this February, 1962, trip around the world, Ethel's aptitude at touch football was utilized more often than her growing linguistic skills. At Waseda University in Tokyo, a Japanese cheer leader accidentally bopped her in the midsection. In Rome, she was challenged to ride a motor scooter and accepted, but unintentionally collided with a small Italian automobile and was knocked to the pavement. Then, during a visit with Queen Juliana of the Netherlands, a palace employee slammed a car door on Ethel's knee. She limped, but insisted she was not hurt.

Just as Robert's older brother and sister, Joe and Kathleen, helped him and his brothers and sisters in training for maturity, their two namesakes among his children have assumed the same role.

"Kathleen and Joe are of great assistance with the younger ones," Ethel Kennedy says. "Kathleen especially likes to help them in their schoolwork as well as read to them and encourage them to learn good manners. Joe is the best one about playing with them and looking out for them so they won't get into trouble, especially when there are no grownups around."

Operating strategically from her current position as wife of the Attorney General and sister-in-law to the President, Ethel Kennedy could, if ambition dictated, reign as the capital's number-one hostess next to the First Lady herself. Ethel possesses a rare combination of unaffected charm, big money, intelligence, a beautiful home, and intimate White House contacts that must stir envy in the party-loving old hearts of Perle Mesta and Gwen Cafritz. But the Attorney General's wife has no inclination to challenge these ladies nor any other contenders for the synthetic title of Washington party-giver supreme.

The Kennedys like to entertain and do so in a folksy, effortless manner. Even formal parties at Hickory Hill reel with informality. When the Kennedys celebrated their eleventh wedding anniversary in June, 1961, guests arrived at the indicated hour in their best summer finery. Before the evening was over, however, Ted Kennedy was pushing them into the swimming pool and plunging in himself. One who got dunked in this fashion was the Attorney General's secretary, Angela Novello. When Angie straggled out of the pool, soaked, shivering and appalled at the sight of her party gown, Ted, equally wet and cold, insisted that she dance with him. She did. The next morning, she received a huge bouquet of red roses from Ted.

Pierre Salinger, now White House press secretary, got a similar impromptu bath a few summers ago. Salinger, then an investigator for the Senate Rackets Committee, was standing at pool side innocently puffing a cigar when Robert Kennedy gave him a shove. Five seconds later, the short, heavy-set Salinger floated to the water's surface like a baby whale, a stoic expression on his face and the cigar still between his teeth.

These frivolous antics rarely escape the society columns of Washington's three daily newspapers and create a general impression that the Kennedys still are a juvenile lot despite the fact that one brother is President of the United States, a second is in the Cabinet, and the third, Ted, is preparing to seek public office in Massachusetts. Actually, the Attorney General does not indulge in such pranks the way he used to and the President has avoided them for years. The Kennedy capers, which make good cocktail party gossip in Washington, belie the fact that a considerable segment of the nation's business is discussed and sometimes transacted in the Georgian manor at Hickory Hill, which was occupied by Jack and Jacqueline Kennedy before the Robert Kennedys moved in. The Attorney General frequently confers in the privacy of his home with his own subordinates from the Department of Justice and with officials from other areas of John Kennedy's administration. It was at Hickory Hill also that he wrote *The Enemy Within*.

The Kennedys strive to keep the atmosphere of their home much as it was in the various homes of Joseph P. Kennedy—in Massachusetts, New York, Palm Beach, London—in those years when Robert himself was growing up in an exciting household with eight brothers and sisters.

While Joe and Rose Kennedy have said they had no special formula for child-rearing, certain tenets were followed. Children were encouraged to think and to do for themselves. They were considered responsible members of the household. Their parents were interested in what they did, and encouraged them to play to win. The children were shown by parental behavior that religious worship is a daily practice, not an occasional attitude.

The pattern is much the same in Robert Kennedy's household. "One of the great things about the Kennedy's," Ethel believes, "is their ability to make decisions. As children they were sent on trips by themselves and had to do for themselves. It helps to travel alone and buy your own ticket and make your own reservations. You find out what it means to make a mistake and get a nonstop ticket when you want to get off at a local station."

The unwavering determination that John and Robert Kennedy exhibited in their drive for the White House was derived in large measure from the training and discipline given them by their father. Although Robert attempts to emulate his father as a disciplinarian, friends who frequented Joe Kennedy's home in the twenties and thirties and now visit Hickory Hill report that he is not as tough as his father was.

"We try to give the older children punishment that will benefit them and enrich their lives," explains Ethel, "like being sent to their rooms to read. Sometimes we deprive them of something they like. They also get spanked." If one method of discipline does not work with an individual child, another one is tried.

Like his father, Robert Kennedy is vitally interested in everything his youngsters do and especially in their achievements. Visitors to his office in the austere Department of Justice are delighted to find the walls decorated with small watercolors and drawings, the uninhibited work of the little Kennedys. The Attorney General also makes it a point to get home for dinner two or three nights a week, even though he may have to return to his office for a few more hours of work. Occasionally he sneaks away from the Department and out to Hickory Hill in the late afternoon to romp with the children.

An intriguing aspect of the Kennedy approach to child-raising is their conviction that the questions of children should be answered seriously at the time they are asked and that the youngsters should be exposed to the conversation of adults. When Robert Kennedy was in the midst of running his brother's presidential campaign, he often summoned politicians and assistants to Hickory Hill for campaign conferences. If the little Kennedys happened to wander into a room while strategy was being discussed or decisions made, their father was not chagrined. He would interrupt the business of the moment to answer their questions cheerfully and to listen to their problems. As Attorney General, he adheres to the same practice.

So does his wife. One day when she was being interviewed in the library of her home by reporters, her second oldest son, Bobby, came running in to announce in the most somber fashion: "Our parakeet is going to die."

"How do you know it is going to die?" asked Ethel, switching automatically from the questions of her interviewers to the dilemma that faced Bobby.

The blond little boy, who strongly resembles his father in physical appearance, replied that one of the hired help had told him parakeets must have mates and cannot survive alone. "So we must have another parakeet so ours won't die," said Bobby.

The reporters had been querying Ethel on the differences in the personalities of John and Robert Kennedy and on how they reacted to the election victory the previous November. She now questioned them on the issue of the moment: Can a parakeet live alone? They did not know.

Ethel finally promised Bobby that she would make a further investigation. "If he can't live alone," she told him, "we'll get another parakeet."

After Bobby darted out to take another look at his lonesome bird, Ethel explained: "Bobby rarely climbs into bed without a moth or some kind of bug. He's the naturalist of this family."

"Pets are supposed to be part of a child's education," Ethel explained to her visitors as she dodged her way through a roving menagerie that includes dogs, horses, ponies, a donkey, ducks, geese, pigeons, goats and an assortment of birds. "We expect the children to take care of them. They have charts and get marks for what they do." She conceded, however, that this theory does not always work and their hired man often ends up taking care of the animals.

The Angora goats, like many of the animals, were a gift to the children. "We were horrified when they first arrived and we found out they had to be fed every four hours," Ethel remembered. "A baby would be less trouble. At least babies wear diapers."

One of the favorite pets was a sea lion that shared the Kennedy swimming pool and frolicked on the lawn. But he kept flipping over the fence that surrounds the pool and frightening guests. "It scared most grownups silly," Ethel recalled. "It would flip over the fence and chase women. Once it went all the way to the shopping center."

This excursion to the McLean, Virginia, shopping center, about three-quarters of a mile away, was the adventure that ended the lion's stay at Hickory Hill. "We had to send him to the Washington zoo," Ethel Kennedy said. "We go there to see him sometimes but he pays no attention. He doesn't know us any more."

Ethel has adopted a card file similar to one used by Rose Kennedy to record illnesses, vaccinations and other statistics about each child. Rose Kennedy found her files useful not only when her children were growing up, but later when she campaigned to help elect Jack to the Senate. In the words of one of Jack Kennedy's political associates, she "wowed them" at political gatherings when she exhibited her files and recited little family incidents that they brought to mind.

Ethel Kennedy may very well use her cards in similar fashion some day, for it is almost certain that one or more of the youngsters she and her husband are rearing will follow their father and uncles into public service.

A request for her to explain her goal in the rearing of her children brought this thoughtful response from Ethel: "I want them to be happy and to make others happy and to see they use their particular talents to make a contribution to our country."

Her father-in-law once proposed as a life goal for one of his children: "To be a worthwhile citizen with good judgment and good understanding."

Ethel Kennedy makes no pretense at being involved in the household drudgery required of wives in lower income brackets. By taking advantage of the extra services money can buy, she can entertain on a moment's notice, travel with her husband at the drop of a suggestion, and devote many hours to her children each week.

"The only time I ever did any cooking was the first year we were married," Ethel says. "Bobby was in the University of Virginia and we lived in an adorable little house in Charlottesville. I never did very well at cooking. Mostly it was catastrophic. Once I tried to fix an omelet. I called my sister in Connecticut and asked her how to cook it. She started to tell me, beginning with breaking the eggs, but I said, 'No, I mean what do you do after it already has fallen?' Mostly we ate out."

The Attorney General's wife is equally candid about the legends that surround Hickory Hill, which has an enormous 300-year-old oak growing among the hickory trees. "People say George Washington rode his horse under that oak," she explains in a voice that has a throaty crackle in it. "We don't know if that is true, any more than we know for sure that the house was General McClellan's headquarters during the Civil War."

The décor of the handsome old house over which Ethel presides is a combination of French provincial and lived-in Kennedy. It is a comfortable place in which are jumbled possibly a hundred photographs and paintings of Kennedys, Skakels and their kin. One of the most striking is a large portrait of Jacqueline Kennedy and her sister, Princess Lee Radziwill, done by their artist friend, William Walton. The most prized and priceless works of art at Hickory Hill, however, are two originals painted by an amateur—John F. Kennedy.

"Once Jack, Bobby and Teddy had a contest to see who could paint the best picture," Ethel remembers. "They painted them in secret, and then brought them out for the rest of the family to judge. Teddy won."

Ethel Kennedy also has on display at Hickory Hill a collection of historical letters which she started for Bob shortly after their marriage. Included are letters written by Presidents Jefferson, Jackson, Lincoln and Tyler, General Hancock and Paul Revere. They are intermingled on the walls of the Kennedy home with letters written to Robert by Presidents Hoover and Franklin D. Roosevelt.

Nothing pleases the mistress of Hickory Hill more than to discuss the achievements of her husband and his family. For days after she sat in near zero weather to hear Jack Kennedy's inaugural address, she told friends: "I cry every time I think of that wonderful speech." Of Jacqueline Kennedy, she says: "Jackie is so thoughtful and so well organized."

One disturbing factor in her family life since her husband became a Cabinet member is a longing for that front-row seat where she could share personally in her husband's triumphs and setbacks as she did during the Racket Committee days.

Not long ago the Attorney General and his wife were invited to sit with other Cabinet officers at the head table during a formal dinner given by the Women's National Press Club. Because Robert was so busy with his official duties, he went to the affair directly from his office and Ethel arrived alone from Hickory Hill.

Ethel looked across the crowded reception room and saw him. She hurried over to kiss him, but Robert, who has a typical Kennedy dislike for exhibiting private emotions in public, already had noticed that news photographers were standing by to take their picture. When Ethel got to him, he held her away and motioned toward the photographers. Ethel blushed and turned away. Jacqueline Kennedy, who was guest of honor at the dinner, sensed her embarrassment and put her arms about her sister-in-law. Then Vice President Lyndon Johnson, a gallant Texan and possibly the kissingest man on the Washington scene since Alben Barkley, walked over to Ethel. When she put out her hand to be shaken, he pushed it aside and kissed her on the cheek.

The incident was reported in the Washington newspapers the next day, and Ethel laughingly conceded that that "was one time I wish I could have gone through the floor."

Evenings out for the Robert Kennedys may include professional football, nondepressing films or plays, as well as Washington social events—but little dancing. "Bob's dancing is a joke," his wife confided recently. "Jack can't dance either—but he's fun to dance with."

Ethel admitted to a troublesome deficiency on her own part when it comes to a frequently faced problem. "For some unknown reason, packing Bob's suitcase is a perennial problem. I have a mental block when it comes to getting all the right things in his bag, despite a typewritten check list on a card in his drawer. Invariably he arrives, as he did recently at the Waldorf-Astoria without a cummerbund or suspenders and only half a black tie, or in Portland with two right shoes, or in Cleveland with somebody's tux pants which would have been a tight fit for Jackie Gleason."

Her husband does not let these lapses go unnoticed. "I have a stack of telegrams from various cities reminding me of the omissions," she said. "One time he ended up at Stowe, Vermont, for a weekend of skiing with three pairs of shorts and a bathing suit."

But the Attorney General has a husbandly failing, too, which balances Ethel's failure as a packer of suitcases. The Kennedys moved six times in the first twelve years of marriage, beginning in Charlottesville and then to several homes in the Georgetown area of Washington before reaching McLean. Asked for a suggestion on how to move big households without being submerged in chaos, Ethel Kennedy laughed:

"Do as Bobby does—plan to be out on the West Coast while your spouse moves children, dogs, horses and furniture."

Chapter Six
The Incredible Era

WHEN ROBERT F. KENNEDY INVITED SENATOR JOSEPH R. McCarthy to Charlottesville in the winter of 1950–51 to address the University of Virginia Student Forum, he had not previously met the strange, complicated man from Wisconsin who already was becoming the most controversial public figure of his time.

But Robert knew that McCarthy, like himself a Catholic of Irish ancestry, was no stranger to other members of the Clan Kennedy. When Jack Kennedy was a freshman Congressman from Massachusetts and Joe McCarthy a freshman Senator from Wisconsin in the 80th Congress, they debated the virtues of the then-pending Taft-Ellender-Wagner Public Housing Bill on nationwide radio—Kennedy for; McCarthy against. McCarthy had dated Patricia Kennedy when she visited in Washington with Jack and her older sister, Eunice. Joseph P. Kennedy knew McCarthy, liked him, supported his campaign against internal communism and had been his host at Hyannisport. McCarthy also was on his way to becoming a national hero in Irish Catholic Boston.

When McCarthy went to Charlottesville at Robert Kennedy's invitation, he had just come through the most amazing and successful year of his life up to that time. It began, much to McCarthy's own amazement, after he claimed in Wheeling, West Virginia, on February 9, 1950, that the State Department was infiltrated with Communists. It ended with the defeat of two of the most powerful Democrats in the United States Senate, Scott Lucas of Illinois and Millard Tydings of Maryland, after McCarthy charged that they were soft on communism.

No one knows exactly what McCarthy said in Wheeling or just what figures he used, because he himself never seemed certain about it. At various times he claimed there were 205, 81 or 57 "known Communists" in the State Department, and sometimes he changed their designation to "bad security risks." But whatever figures or descriptions he cited that night, they launched Joe McCarthy on one of the most dazzling and dizzy political adventures in the history of the United States. Through much of it—both the triumphs and the inevitable tragedy—Robert Kennedy was either a participant or a front-row spectator.

Through the next seven years, Robert Kennedy was to become and remain a personal friend of McCarthy. But Kennedy also was destined in those same years to take sharp issue with the senator's investigative techniques and his conduct as committee chairman.

It was Robert's purpose in his last year at the University of Virginia to reinvigorate the old student forum by bringing to the campus men who were prominent, controversial and whose views covered the shades of the political spectrum. The vast contacts that his father and his brother had among public men helped him achieve this goal with smashing success. Certainly in that period there was no bigger catch for the speaker's platform than Joe McCarthy. He probably was in greater demand than even the President of the United States, Harry S. Truman, or the leader of the Republican right, Senator Robert A. Taft of Ohio.

Robert Kennedy remembers that when he met Joe McCarthy for the first time at the university, "I liked him almost immediately." The feeling was mutual and it was one that did not change, even when the two men sat on opposite sides of the wildest Congressional free-for-all ever staged, the nationally televised Army-McCarthy hearings of 1954.

"He always was so nice to me," says Kennedy. "I never had any personal disputes with him."

When Robert Kennedy was graduated from law school, the summer after his first meeting with McCarthy, he entered the Department of Justice and was assigned to a good spot in the Internal Security Division. He felt that the United States faced a threat from internal as well as external communism and that it should be combated. The Internal Security Division was the logical place to fight communism, and Bob was there when McCarthy developed the biggest case of his flamboyant career—that of Owen Lattimore.

In March, 1950, McCarthy, then being hounded by the Senate's Tydings Committee to prove the accusations he had made about Communists in government, announced that he had uncovered the identity of the "top Russian espionage agent" in the nation. A few days later he announced that this man was Owen Lattimore, Johns Hopkins University professor, expert on Far Eastern matters, a writer and a public sympathizer with Red causes. He contended that Lattimore was the chief architect of the Truman Administration's China policy and was "Alger Hiss's boss in the espionage ring in the State Department."

When Robert Kennedy arrived at the Justice Department, the Internal Security Division was busily investigating and sifting McCarthy's charges and Lattimore's denials. Although Kennedy was busy on a variety of espionage cases, he did not participate in the Lattimore case.

Actively involved in the Lattimore case, however, was another bright, ambitious young attorney named Roy M. Cohn. It is one of the interesting sidelights of history that Robert Kennedy and Roy Cohn both worked on espionage cases in the Internal Security Division at the same time without ever meeting.

Yet within two years these two young lawyers would be performing a bitter two-man sideshow to the great McCarthy Communist Spy Carnival.

After his brief interlude with the Lattimore case, Kennedy was assigned to another area of investigation that was proving particularly troublesome to the Government in those days—corruption. He was one of three attorneys named to probe the misdoings of Truman Administration officials, and played a major role in laying before a Brooklyn grand jury the case against Commissioner of Internal Revenue Joseph Nunan.

Through this period when Robert Kennedy was learning something of law and investigative procedures in the Department of Justice, John Kennedy was dashing home to Massachusetts from Washington at every possible opportunity to mend his political fences in preparation for the 1952 senatorial race. Finally, early in the election year, he officially entered the race against Senator Henry Cabot Lodge, a Republican Brahmin who was thought unbeatable in Massachusetts, especially after he had successfully piloted General of the Army Dwight D. Eisenhower to the GOP presidential nomination at the national party convention in Chicago that year.

As Jack Kennedy plunged into the uphill race against Lodge, his brother plunged in beside him as campaign manager. Behind Robert Kennedy was the less exhilarating life of attorney in the Justice Department. As his brother's chief of staff in the Senate race, he taught seasoned and successful politicians a few tricks of campaigning they never knew existed and occasionally ordered them about like recruits. He began to develop the reputation that since has spread across the land—that of a pugnacious and hard-headed little guy who relentlessly pursues his goal, letting heads fall where they may.

In Massachusetts, as at the University of Virginia and in the nation's capital, Robert Kennedy once more came upon the fascinating figure of Joseph R. McCarthy. McCarthy was big in the Bay State and especially in Boston. He also was storming about the country campaigning for all Republicans who would have him, including General Ike. It was quite probable that McCarthy, with his huge following among Irish

Catholics who for years had voted Democratic, could determine the outcome of the Massachusetts senatorial election. There were rumors that Old Joe Kennedy made a huge contribution to Joe McCarthy's campaign that year to keep him out of Massachusetts. But the former Ambassador dismissed this accusation as "baloney" when he was interviewed by *The Saturday Evening Post* writer Joe McCarthy (no relation to the Senator) for his book *The Remarkable Kennedys.*

The elder Kennedy said: "I gave Joe McCarthy a small contribution, sure, but it was only a couple of thousand dollars and I didn't give it to him to keep him out of Massachusetts. I gave it to him because a mutual friend of ours, Westbrook Pegler, asked me to give it to him and because I liked the fight he was putting up against Communists in our government. Nobody had to pay McCarthy to keep him from working for Lodge. There was no love between them. I remember that McCarthy told my son Bobby that year that if the Republican National Committee asked him to speak for them in Massachusetts he would have to do it. They didn't ask him to do it because Lodge didn't want him. If you want my opinion, Lodge made a big mistake. McCarthy would have gotten him a lot of votes."

Despite McCarthy's popularity in Massachusetts, there were heavy liberal pressures on Jack Kennedy to denounce the Wisconsin firebrand who had impugned the loyalty not only of Harry Truman and Adlai E. Stevenson and Dean Acheson, but of the Democratic Party itself.

In his biography of John Kennedy, James MacGregor Burns recites an incident that occurred in Jack's Bowdoin Street apartment across from the Massachusetts State Capitol in Boston, at the height of the senatorial campaign.

Burns says that Gardner (Pat) Jackson, of the CIO, had prepared a strong denouncement of McCarthy and took it to the apartment. Joe Kennedy and other campaign aides were present. Burns tells the rest of the story in this way:

> He [Jackson] got through three sentences when Joseph Kennedy sprang to his feet with such force that he upset a small table in front of him. He stormed over to Jackson almost as if he would attack him.
> "You and your friends are trying to ruin my son's career." He was not opposed to McCarthy, he shouted; he had contributed to his campaign. Again and again he returned to the charge that liberals and union people were hurting his son.

Burns goes on to state that John Kennedy took no part in the argument and left the apartment without any comment to his father or Jackson about the McCarthy issue.

Joe McCarthy, of course, did not campaign in Massachusetts in 1952. Not only did he dislike Lodge, he also had a great fondness for the Kennedys.

When the votes were counted in November, Jack Kennedy had beaten the unbeatable Lodge by 70,000 votes. Robert Kennedy, who ran his brother's campaign so expertly, began once more thinking about his own future.

As the son of a one-time Democratic administration official and ambassador and as the brother of a Democratic congressman, he had fared well in the Justice Department under a Democratic administration. But on the day that Jack Kennedy defeated Lodge, Dwight D. Eisenhower was elected President and the Republicans, for only the second time in twenty-two years, gained control of both houses of Congress.

McCarthy also was re-elected and he was bigger than ever. Although he ran far behind Eisenhower in Wisconsin in 1952, he campaigned cross-country for the GOP and even made a nationwide television speech in which, utilizing innuendo and half truths, he linked the Democratic presidential nominee, Adlai Stevenson, to communism. Because of McCarthy's power with the electorate, Ike omitted from a speech in Wisconsin the praise he planned to speak for his honored mentor, General of the Army George Catlett Marshall. Sherman Adams suggested to Eisenhower that he not laud the great soldier in Wisconsin because local Republican leaders feared it might antagonize McCarthy and his followers. McCarthy, in a long Senate speech in June, 1951, had accused Marshall of being a man "steeped in falsehood"; one who was part of "a conspiracy so immense and an infamy so black as to dwarf any previous venture in the history of man"; a holder of high military and civilian office whose decisions invariably served "the world policy of the Kremlin."

In addition to his victory at the polls and his acquisition of power within the Republican party, McCarthy was about to become chairman of the Senate Committee on Government Operations and its Permanent Subcommittee on Investigations. He had indicated his willingness, immediately after Eisenhower's election, to give up the pursuit of Communists now that the government was in safe Republican hands, and turn instead to graft and corruption. But in a politician's life it often is a long, long time from November to January, and by mid-December McCarthy was finding new Red fronts to conquer.

Still, as Robert Kennedy recalls, McCarthy, during

December, 1952, and January, 1953, painted an impressive picture of the future he had in mind for the committee.

"He said he wanted to reconstruct the committee, to go into all kinds of investigations—communism and elsewhere," says Robert Kennedy. "He wanted to find people who could help him do a good job."

In the quest for such people, Francis (Frip) Flanagan, a former FBI agent who at the time was general counsel to the Permanent Subcommittee on Investigations, contacted James McInerney, Assistant Attorney General in the outgoing Truman Administration and Robert Kennedy's boss at the Justice Department. McInerney recommended Kennedy to Flanagan and Kennedy was anxious to accept the challenge of working for the McCarthy Committee. McCarthy presumably was just as eager to have the alert and energetic son of his friend, Joe Kennedy, on his staff. Robert Kennedy maintains, however, that he went to the committee because he believed there was a job to be done and not from personal consideration for McCarthy. "I felt the investigation of communism was an important domestic issue," he says.

At the same time that Kennedy went to work under Flanagan, McCarthy hired Roy Cohn as chief counsel for the subcommittee. Cohn, son of a Democratic chieftain in the Bronx, had helped prosecute atomic spies Julius and Ethel Rosenberg while working in the office of the U. S. Attorney in New York. He brought with him to the subcommittee the rich young heir to a hotel chain fortune, G. David Schine. Schine, who had the title "chief consultant," once had written a brief tract called "Definition of Communism" which seemed to have been distributed in his family's hotels the way Gideon Bibles were in other hotels.

Here began a feud that to this day can elicit some

of the more basic expletives from Robert Kennedy, who, as his wife Ethel explains, "never forgets."

"That was an incredible era," says Kennedy of the two years of the 83rd Congress when the accusations, the adventures, and the investigations of McCarthy, Cohn and Schine were making florid headlines with each successive edition of the nation's newspapers.

In the beginning things were not too bad for Robert Kennedy. He and Cohn never got along, but in his initial assignments on the subcommittee he served under Flanagan. His biggest job in this period was an investigation of East-West trade that produced some startling results, including angry denunciations of young Kennedy by the British.

Testifying before the McCarthy Subcommittee, investigator Kennedy said that in 1952, while U. S. boys were fighting communist Chinese soldiers in Korea, 193 ships belonging to Western allied nations traded with Red China on "an absolute minimum" of 445 voyages. In the same year, he said, 66 Western flagships traded at communist ports in Europe.

He also testified that in the first three months of 1953, while the Korean war still was flaming, "an absolute minimum" of 162 Western vessels, 100 of which were British, did business with Red China. Then he added the real shocker: Two ships owned by the British firm of Wheelock-Marden had transported Chinese communist troops.

Senator John McClellan of Arkansas contended that Kennedy's statistics proved that Britain's trade with the Peking regime at least equaled or possibly offset its contributions to the Korean war. McCarthy said: "It seems unbelievable, unheard of . . . that a nation would have ships owned by its nationals transporting the troops to kill its own soldiers."

The Wheelock-Marden Company branded Kennedy's charges "a horrible lie" and the British Embassy called them "fantastic."

But Kennedy and Flanagan stuck to their guns and *The New York Times* columnist Arthur Krock said the probe was "an example of Congressional investigation at its highest."

On his first tour of duty with the McCarthy Subcommittee, Robert Kennedy lasted six months. He found working on the same staff with Roy Cohn and Dave Schine exceedingly difficult. But when McCarthy made Cohn chief counsel in June, 1953, he found it intolerable.

In some ways Robert Kennedy and Roy Cohn were young men alike. Both came from prominent families and had been given good educations. Both were in their middle twenties when they clashed. Both had served in the Justice Department. Both were intelligent and aggressive and possessed of explosive dispositions. Both had to some degree arrived at their anti-Communist stand because of religion.

In his critical profile of Joe McCarthy, Richard Rovere states:

> In all probability, Cohn's anti-communism was somewhat less of a caprice and an improvisation than McCarthy's, for Cohn was Jewish and from New York, and at about the time he came to man's estate and participated in the Rosenberg prosecution, it seemed terribly important to many Jews not only to disassociate themselves from Jewish Communists, but to demonstrate a zealous and fiery anti-communism. His Jewishness, indeed, was one of the things that qualified him for a part in the Rosenberg case—in which, by prearrangement, the entire prosecuting staff and the judge were Jews.

Robert Kennedy undoubtedly was influenced in his anti-communist views by his Catholicism. The McCarthy era coincided with a time of great distress among American Catholics, who viewed the march of communism as a mortal threat to both their nation and their church. They freshly had seen their clergy, their missionaries and their fellow laymen suffer in lands subdued by communism—Poland, Hungary, Czechoslovakia, China and the rest. It was the fear of communism, fanned on one hand by the agitation of the McCarthyites and on the other by the cavalier negligence of the Trumanites, that caused a good share of the exodus of Catholics from the Democratic to the Republican party in 1950 and 1952.

McCarthy was successful for quite a period at making a good many of his fellow Irish Catholics believe that he alone in the United States perceived their double fear and could save both church and nation. Robert Kennedy obviously did not accept this, but he did support McCarthy's basic theory that Communists had to be ferreted out of the government. He also admired McCarthy's loyalty to his staff—up to a point.

In his book, *The Enemy Within,* Kennedy points out that congressional investigators have come to expect "little or no support" from their bosses, the committee members. He explains that senators and congressmen can be ruthless in using staff-gathered information for their own personal political advantage and in firing investigators for simple first mistakes.

"These fears are not unjustified," writes Kennedy. "The record will show that, aside from Senator McCarthy—one of whose greatest mistakes was that he was loyal beyond reason to Roy Cohn and G. David Schine—congressional committee members as a rule have been unwilling to stand up and be counted on behalf of a staff member who meets difficulty."

In those first six months on the Investigations Sub-committee, Robert Kennedy was appalled at the conduct of Cohn and Schine and at the way in which McCarthy permitted them to operate the subcommittee. While McCarthy indulged himself in headlines and radio-television appearances, the sallow-faced, combative Cohn ran the subcommittee with the handsome, less clever Schine as his helpmate.

First they conducted a widely heralded investigation of the Voice of America which damaged employee morale within that vital propaganda arm of America's foreign policy and left the nationwide impression that it was a wholly discredited agency, filled with Communists, homosexuals and fuzzy-minded fellow travelers. There probably was substance to some of what Cohn and Schine were trying to prove, but almost all substance was lost in the performance put on with tumult and tragedy by the two young investigators before the nation's television cameras.

Next they went on a whirlwind "book burning" expedition through the capitals of Europe. Through Paris, Bonn, Frankfurt, Munich, Vienna, Belgrade, Athens, Rome and London, the two precocious youngsters romped in search of books by Communists, alleged Communists, or suspected Communists in the libraries of the International Information Administration. It was one of the most raucous farces ever performed on European soil by Americans—and Europe rejoiced to every prat-fall, every corny line, every concocted bit of intrigue.

McCarthy seemed not at all dismayed. He publicly defended his boys and even claimed they were victims of vicious anti-Semitism. It didn't matter to Joe that many of the most vocal opponents of the McCarthy-Cohn-Schine operation were themselves Jews—like

New York's Senator Herbert Lehman and *New York Post* Editor James Weschler.

Joe McCarthy's fantastic world began to disintegrate in the summer of 1953, but it is doubtful that he was aware of it at the time.

In June of that year, he elevated Cohn to chief counsel. After the Voice of America probe, the ludicrous junket through Europe and scores of minor incidents, this was too much for the Democratic members of the committee—Senators John McClellan of Arkansas, Stuart Symington of Missouri, and Henry Jackson of Washington. They walked out on McCarthy and announced they would not return until they could have a hand in determining who would serve on the subcommittee staff.

It also was too much for Robert Kennedy. By that time he had built up a bitter dislike for Cohn and a contempt for Schine, and he knew it would not be possible to serve under them. In his book, he explains: "I told McCarthy that I disagreed with the way the committee was being run, except for the work that Flanagan had done, and that the way they were proceeding I thought it was headed for disaster."

Kennedy feels as strongly today as he did then that Cohn and Schine—with their trip through Europe and later Cohn's attempts to get special treatment from the Army for Schine—"were major factors in giving congressional committees a black eye from which they have not yet fully recovered."

He says in his book that under McCarthy, with Cohn and Schine, "most of the investigations were instituted on the basis of some preconceived notion by the chief counsel or his staff members and not on the basis of any information that had been developed. Cohn and Schine claimed they knew from the outset what was

wrong; and they were not going to let the facts inter-
fere. Therefore no real spade work that might have destroyed some of their pet theories was ever undertaken.
I thought Senator McCarthy made a mistake in allow-
ing the committee to operate in such a fashion, told
him so and resigned."

Kennedy says the longest and most serious conversation he ever had with McCarthy was on the day in the
summer of 1953 when he informed the Senator that he
was leaving the committee.

"I told him I thought he was out of his mind and
was going to destroy himself," says Kennedy. "He disliked Schine and said he was going to get rid of him.
He asked me to stay on for a month. But I said I would
have to resign. But he kept me on the payroll for a
month."

Within a few weeks after Kennedy and the trio of
Democratic senators walked out on McCarthy, Schine
got a draft notice from the Army, Cohn began maneu-
vering to get Dave preferential treatment, and Mc-
Carthy was on his way to his violent clash with the
Army, Senate censure and self-ruin.

Kennedy went from the McCarthy Committee to
the Commission on the Organization of the Executive
Branch of the Government—the Hoover Commission—
on which his father was serving as a member.

For eight months he worked with former President
Herbert Hoover, helping him organize the commission.
"I greatly admired him," says Kennedy. "Most of the
time, there were not many people around and so I had
a chance to work with and talk with him personally. It
was a wonderful experience."

Although he had been exposed to public men all his
life, he found that Hoover "had a greater knowledge
of government generally than any man I'd ever
known."

Robert Kennedy found his association with the former president exhilarating, but he found the work dull and saw no real future in what he was doing. Friends and family report that this was the toughest period in his life. One close friend recalls: "Bobby went through a terribly difficult time before the McClellan Committee began. He wanted to achieve. He had proved himself in the 1952 election, but he wasn't able to find anything to get his teeth into. The McCarthy era was frustrating. There were many clashes with Roy Cohn. But even that period was more interesting than the one that followed—the one on the Hoover Commission. He was dissatisfied with the Hoover Commission. He was rather cross much of the time in those days, with his family, and his friends. Bob normally is one of the most pleasant persons to be around. But he just wasn't himself in that period. . . ."

After eight months with the Hoover Commission, Bob returned to the McCarthy Subcommittee at the request of McClellan, Jackson and Symington as their minority counsel. He worked for the three Democrats —all men of integrity and ability—and not for Cohn.

He carried away from the Hoover Commission some prized memories of working side by side with a man in whom he saw greatness and a letter from the 31st President of the United States, saying: "I realize . . . that there is little to do until the task forces have reported and that a restless soul like you wants to work."

Back on the McCarthy Subcommittee, Bob's disputes with Cohn continued but were possibly even more violent than before. Cohn especially was angered when during the interrogation of one Annie Lee Moss, a Negro employee of the Army Signal Corps who had been identified as a Communist party member, Kennedy exposed Cohn's slipshod investigative practices.

Mrs. Moss denied ever having been a member of the Communist party, but she did recall that a man named Rob Hall had delivered the *Daily Worker* to her home once. Cohn had based much of his case on the fact that this was the same Robert Hall who was a top communist organizer in the District of Columbia.

Cohn said at an open hearing on March 10, 1954, that "we felt there was significance in the fact that Robert Hall had come to the home of Mrs. Moss and persuaded her or somebody in the house to subscribe to the *Daily Worker*."

After Mrs. Moss mentioned that the Rob Hall who called at her home was a Negro, one of the newspaper reporters covering the hearing tipped Kennedy off that the Communist Rob Hall was white. This colloquy followed:

MR. KENNEDY. Was Mr. Hall a colored gentleman, or—

MRS. MOSS. Yes, sir.

MR. KENNEDY. There is some confusion about it, is there not, Mr. Cohn? Is the Rob Hall we are talking about, the union organizer, was he a white man or a colored man?

MR. COHN. I never inquired into his race. I am not sure. We can check that, though.

MR. KENNEDY. I thought I just spoke to you about it.

MR. COHN. My assumption has been that he is a white man, but we can check that.

SENATOR SYMINGTON. Let us ask this: The Bob Hall that you knew, was he a white man?

MRS. MOSS. He was colored, the one I knew of.

SENATOR SYMINGTON. Let's decide which Robert Hall we want to talk about.

MR. KENNEDY. When you spoke about the union organizer, you spoke about Rob Hall and I think we all felt that was the colored gentleman?

MR. COHN. I was not talking about a union organizer, Bob. I was talking about a communist organizer who at that time, according to public record, was in charge of subscriptions for the *Daily Worker* in the District of Columbia area.

MR. KENNEDY. Evidently it is a different Rob Hall.

MR. COHN. I don't know that it is. Our information is that it was the same Rob Hall.

SENATOR MCCLELLAN. If one is black and the other is white, there is a difference.

MR. COHN. I think that might better be something we should go into and get some more exact information on.

MR. KENNEDY. I think so too.

There were disputes between Kennedy and Cohn behind the committee scenes that reporters overheard.

On one occasion, Senator Jackson exposed the weaknesses of Cohn-Schine investigative techniques in a public hearing. When the session ended, the irate Cohn stormed up to Kennedy. "You tell your friend, Scoop Jackson, we're going to get him on Monday," said Cohn, intimating that he had material out of the past that would reflect on Jackson.

"Get lost," retorted Kennedy.

Joe McCarthy, still possessed of a large and fanatical public following, now was in full-scale combat with the United States Army. He already had taken on two presidents—Truman and Eisenhower—and fared rather well against them. There was no reason why the Army should be more difficult.

The problem, however, was not so much that the

swaggering, reckless McCarthy had met his match in the Army as that he had met it in the people of the United States. Some twenty million strong, they sat before their television sets each day in the late spring and early summer of 1954 watching the strange proceedings on Capitol Hill. Many found themselves for the first time shocked and outraged by McCarthy's brutal surliness and his bullying of fellow senators, Pentagon officials and lesser witnesses.

In the opening lines of his book Richard Rovere describes McCarthy in this way: "The late Joseph R. McCarthy, a United States senator from Wisconsin, was in many ways the most gifted demagogue ever bred on these shores. No bolder seditionist ever moved among us—nor any politician with a surer, swifter access to the dark places of the American mind."

McCarthy was likened by many of his antagonists, including Mrs. Eleanor Roosevelt, to Adolf Hitler, and some of his techniques were remarkably like those of the power-mad house painter who ignited World War II. But if there was something of Hitler in him, there also were large chunks of Sinclair Lewis's charming charlatan, "Elmer Gantry," and Arthur Miller's pitiful salesman, "Willy Loman." Like Gantry, he was a dynamic evangelist who reveled in the phoniness of his endeavors. Like Willy Loman—whose philosophy was "be liked and you will never want"—McCarthy sought the favor and admiration of his fellow man, but never quite attained them in the amounts he required.

The accusations were so bold, the personalities so colorful, the conflict so fierce that most of the public never really knew what the Army-McCarthy hearings were all about. The battle began with Cohn's fanatical attempts—backed by the power and prestige of McCarthy himself—to get preferential treatment for Schine who was about to enter the Army. Cohn sought a commission for Schine. When that failed, he went after special assignments for him. He tried to get Schine into the Central Intelligence Agency so that he could avoid military service altogether. After Schine was inducted, Cohn got him an immediate two-week furlough, ostensibly to work for the subcommittee. Army Secretary Robert T. Stevens in turn attempted to appease McCarthy and Cohn by granting special privileges to Schine in hopes that the subcommittee would call off a projected security probe of Fort Monmouth. Involved on the sidelines was Brigadier General Ralph Zwicker who was insulted viciously by McCarthy behind closed doors for his role in promoting a dentist, Major Irving Peress, whom McCarthy linked to communism.

When the whole sordid shebang had ended, Robert Kennedy performed the most creditable and constructive feat to come out of the Army-McCarthy hearings. During the hearings, Kennedy had prepared questions for Democratic members of the committee and had played what he regards as a major role in preventing the abuse of witnesses. With the investigation at an end, he prepared a seventy-eight-page summary of evidence—a detailed fact sheet—that was accepted by both Republicans and Democrats. This was a monumental accomplishment, considering the deep bitterness caused by the controversy. To the summary of evidence, the Republican majority, the Democratic minority, and individual senators on the subcommittee attached their diverse views.

While Kennedy still was working on the summary, Senator Ralph Flanders, a Vermont Republican, launched the attack that was to kill McCarthy and cause political embarrassment for John Kennedy. Flanders introduced on the Senate floor on July 30, 1954, a resolution of censure against McCarthy. The resolution was debated at length and then the Senate named a Select Committee under Senator Arthur Watkins, a Utah Republican and Mormon elder, to sift the charges against McCarthy. On December 2, the Senate, by a vote of 67 to 22, voted to condemn McCarthy on two counts: for contempt of the Senate Committee on Privileges and Elections during its 1952 probe of the Wisconsin Senator's strange finances and for abuse of the Watkins Committee in 1954.

While the Watkins Committee was conducting its hearings, Robert Kennedy and Senator Jackson—Scoop —were in the Pacific Northwest on a fishing trip. Jack Kennedy still was confined to a hospital following back surgery.

But Jack Kennedy was haunted right up to the 1960 Democratic national convention by liberal suspicions of him because of his failure to take a stand on McCarthy, although at the time of the censure vote he was critically ill in Florida following a back operation and had been given the last rites of the Catholic Church. After his overwhelming re-election in Massachusetts in 1958, Kennedy did say that he had prepared a speech on the Flanders resolution in the summer of 1954, but had not given it because the Senate—with him voting in the affirmative—agreed to appoint the Watkins Committee to hear charges against McCarthy.

In that speech, which was made public in 1959, Jack Kennedy said he would vote to censure McCarthy, not because of McCarthy's actions toward the Privileges and Elections Committee in a previous Congress, nor because of the Wisconsin Senator's deplorable treatment of Zwicker, but because of the abusive language and threats of reprisal used against the Army by Roy Cohn and acquiesced in by McCarthy. He said that McCarthy, as chairman of the Permanent Investigations Subcommittee, had to take full responsibility for the conduct of his staff. Robert Kennedy helped his brother prepare the speech and agreed with the position it stated.

When Robert Kennedy first went to work for the McCarthy subcommittee, Joe Kennedy was all in favor of the move, but Jack opposed it. Long after McCarthy had been censured and had died a broken man, Jack Kennedy explained why he could not vote for censure based on McCarthy's conduct toward the Privileges and Elections Committee in 1952. James MacGregor Burns quotes him as saying: "So I was rather in ill grace personally to be around hollering about what McCarthy had done in 1952 when my brother had been on the staff in 1953. That is really the guts of the matter."

By the time McCarthy was censured, the nation had once more been to the polls and the Democrats had recaptured the two houses of Congress. John McClellan became chairman of the Government Operations Committee and the Permanent Investigations Subcommittee and Robert Kennedy became chief counsel. McCarthy was simply the ranking member.

In that period, McCarthy proved an important ally to both McClellan and Kennedy. While the other Republicans, Senator Karl Mundt of North Dakota and the late Senator George Bender of Ohio, attempted to exact every ounce of political flesh from the subcommittee's operations, McCarthy co-operated with McClellan and was of great assistance to him in his attempts to keep the subcommittee's activities above narrow partisanship. He likewise supported Robert Kennedy in his bouts with Mundt, who seemed set on getting rid of the rich boy from Boston whom he rather intensely disliked. McCarthy almost invariably bypassed his own minority counsel, James Juliana, and went to Kennedy to learn what was happening on the committee and to make suggestions about investigations.

When in February, 1957, the Senate Select Committee on Improper Activities in Labor Management Field (the Rackets Committee) was established, McClellan and Senator Sam Ervin, a canny and humorous old North Carolina Democrat, insisted that McCarthy be given a seat on it. Once more McCarthy and Robert Kennedy worked together. But the end was very near for Joe. He drank so heavily that at times he was almost incoherent in talking with senators and reporters. He made only token stabs at being his old flamboyant self during interrogation. He talked grandly of laying before the public a scandalous story of skulduggery in Walter Reuther's United Auto Workers Union, but his lassitude, his badly failing health and his addiction to the bottle all combined to make this impossible.

At 6:02 on the evening of May 2, 1957, the end came in the Naval Medical Center in Bethesda, Maryland, for Joseph R. McCarthy—a man despised, a man idolized, a man feared as the destroyer of freedom and liberty, a man revered as a messiah come to save a nation, a cruel and abusive man, a thoughtful and likable man.

While Robert Kennedy does not agree with Richard Rovere's harsh assessment of McCarthy, he does agree with Rovere that the day McCarthy hired Cohn and Schine he sealed his doom.

"He got so involved with all the publicity—and after that it was the number one thing in his life," says Kennedy. "He was on a toboggan. It was so exciting and exhilarating as he went downhill that it didn't matter to him if he hit a tree at the bottom.

"Cohn and Schine took him up the mountain and

showed him all those wonderful things. He destroyed himself for that—for publicity. He had to get his name in the paper. I felt sorry for him, particularly in the last year, when he was such a beaten, destroyed person —particularly since many of his so-called friends, realizing he was finished, ran away from him and left him with virtually no one."

It is difficult for the legion of Americans who so bitterly hated McCarthy to think that anyone with an ounce of liberalism in them could like him or sympathize with him. Yet, strangely enough, a number of his most fiery opponents in Washington had a personal liking for McCarthy. He had an unaffected, almost childish, charm about him. He could not quite understand why some people were so violent against him, when he himself viewed so much of what he was doing as a fabulously entertaining game—one to be played like jousting, for excitement and fun, and what matter if blood spilled now and then?

"I liked him and yet at times he was terribly heavy handed," says Robert Kennedy. "He was a very complicated character. His whole method of operation was complicated because he would get a guilty feeling and get hurt after he had blasted somebody. He wanted so desperately to be liked. He was so thoughtful and yet so unthoughtful in what he did to others. He was sensitive and yet insensitive. He didn't anticipate the results of what he was doing. He was very thoughtful of his friends, and yet he could be so cruel to others."

Yet Kennedy is convinced that had he sat in the United States Senate in 1954, he would have had to vote to censure McCarthy. "I thought he had brought the Senate and the United States into disrepute by his operation of the committee," explains Kennedy. "The whole operation of Cohn and Schine was the core of it. To censure him for not appearing before a committee [the Privileges and Elections Committee] prior to his re-election, or because of what he said about other senators [on the Watkins Committee] was not so significant."

For all his weaknesses and his craving for the spotlight, Joe McCarthy could have avoided censure by the Senate "if he had handled himself differently," says Robert Kennedy.

When the final rites were read for Joseph R. McCarthy in St. Mary's Catholic Church in Appleton, Wisconsin, on May 7, 1957, there was seated in the choir loft a slight, solemn young man whose head was bowed in meditation. This was Robert F. Kennedy, come to say farewell to the complicated man who had been so nice to him.

Chapter Seven
The Cherry Trees Are Safe

ONCE EACH YEAR, ON THE DAY WHEN THE NATION COM- memorates the birthday of George Washington, the elegant, classically constructed capital city named for the first President is converted into a frenzied carnival of commercialism.

The departments of government and most nonretail businesses are closed, ostensibly to honor the squire of Mount Vernon but more realistically to permit employees to chase a cut-rate rainbow. Many hours before stores are to open, rabid bargain seekers, swathed in woolens, long johns and blankets and fortified with hot coffee and warm whisky, begin to queue up along downtown streets in the cold darkness of winter night. All await the golden morning hour of nine o'clock when doors of specialty shops and discount houses first crack open. The eager customers then burst in upon harried clerks and grasp onto ninety-nine-cent television sets, eighty-eight-cent dresses and other weirdly priced sales items.

Although the city lay under a near-paralyzing siege of ice and frigid temperatures and John F. Kennedy had just demanded sacrifice and austerity on the New Frontier, the spending orgy was no less frantic or depreciative of George Washington on February 22, 1961, than in previous years. The capital of the world was for a few sordid hours one giant bargain basement.

But Robert F. Kennedy and the ambitious young men who had moved into the Department of Justice with him just one month earlier did not regard the holiday as either a time for buying or a time for relaxation. They showed up at their desks at the proper hour.

The Attorney General had not requested other employees to work that day. When his black Cadillac limousine rolled into the courtyard at the Department, however, Kennedy was pleased to note that the cars of many civil servants already were there.

Although Robert Kennedy possesses an abundant capacity for play and thrives on vigorous summer weekends at Cape Cod and equally active winter weekends on the ski slopes of New England or the sands of Palm Beach, he never has limited his working schedule to an eight-hour, five-day week. When a job has to be done, he regards late night, early morning, Saturdays, Sundays and holidays as being just as conducive to hard work as the hours from nine to five-thirty, Monday through Friday.

The Attorney General, therefore, felt there should be some reward for others within his departmental jurisdiction who had shown a devotion to duty on a Federal holiday. He obtained a list of all persons who had parked their cars in the courtyard that day, and wrote personal letters of gratitude to every one. In the letters he stated that their devotion to duty on Washington's Birthday was "the attitude we need at Justice."

Kennedy had not reckoned with the possibility that some of his devoted employees might have used the courtyard strictly for parking purposes while pursuing bargains in nearby stores.

Shortly after his letters had been distributed, Kennedy received a reply from an employee named John T. Sharpnoch. Sharpnoch thanked Kennedy for his thoughtfulness, but explained: "In keeping with the spirit of Washington's birthday, I must 'confess' that I did not work on that day."

The Attorney General was delighted by this display of integrity. His reply was immediate and in the same light vein.

"With honesty like this in the Department, the nation's cherry trees are safe," he wrote to Sharpnoch.

The incident is characteristic of the spirit of energy and informal fraternity that young Robert Kennedy brought into one of the five original departments of government, established in 1789, the year that Washington became President.

Immediately upon assuming the duties of Attorney General, he began drifting in and out of Department offices—greeting employees with an outstretched hand, a smile and a statement of fact: "I'm Bob Kennedy."

Employee morale is a constant dilemma in a sprawling government operation like the Department of Justice. There are within its framework hundreds of men and women who for twenty or thirty or forty years have reported to the same desk in the same little office each morning and gone home each evening without receiving any recognition beyond a biweekly pay check.

Many of these individuals caught on the bureaucratic treadmill were disturbed by the prospect of falling under the rule of Robert Kennedy. For he had been preceded into the Department by his campaign reputation as a brash, autocratic little rich boy who administered the *coup de grâce* without feeling to all who stood in the path of his brother's climb to the Presidency.

Robert Kennedy can be brash and he can be autocratic. He places heavy demands upon those who serve him. But he also has a faculty for igniting tremendous loyalty among his employees because he refuses to spare himself when there is a goal to be achieved and because he possesses an infectious boyish charm and a thoughtfulness that runs deeper than the dedication of many wealthy persons to the ancient principle of noblesse oblige.

As a start toward a more efficient and harmonious Department, Kennedy sought to make long-time civil servants realize that they had a friend in the front office who was interested in them as individuals and who appreciated their services and needed their help.

The move was in direct contrast to the misguided conduct of some of President Eisenhower's Cabinet officers who believed their 1952 campaign oratory about cleaning out the government "from the top down" and entered Federal service with a basic distrust of all who had worked in the departments and agencies under the New Deal and Fair Deal. It took many months of stumbling before these men came to realize that their burdens could be lightened and their knowledge broadened by those anonymous souls who had made the U. S. Government their career.

There should be no inference that Kennedy's immediate predecessor, former Attorney General William Rogers, was guilty of such callous behavior. Rogers is a gentleman of great personal charm and democratic instincts, who knew and understood government before entering the Department of Justice as Deputy Attorney General in 1953. He also was not elevated to Attorney General until the second term of the Eisenhower Administration.

During his first few weeks as Attorney General, Robert Kennedy staged a series of get-togethers in his own office, meeting in groups of forty all employees who had been with the Department more than fifteen years and all three hundred law school honor graduates serving apprenticeships there.

One man who had been working at Justice for twenty years confided that his only previous brush with an Attorney General had been a brief introduction to Herbert Brownell at a cocktail party.

Kennedy attached special significance to his meetings with the law school honor graduates. Many of them were not much younger than the Attorney General himself and he felt they should be encouraged to remain in the Department instead of following a pattern of drifting into private practice after less than two years' service in the government.

Kennedy scored in the delicate area of personnel relations, but the political woods are filled with has-beens who were popular with their employees but failures as administrators and policy makers.

Except for a brief question and answer exchange with the Senate Judiciary Committee during his confirmation hearing on January 13, 1961, he had shed little light on the course he planned to follow as the nation's chief legal and law-enforcement officer. There were serious doubts as to where he stood on the most critical question within his domain—civil rights.

Then, one day in the early spring of 1961, a door opened. And through it walked a University of Georgia Law School student named Jay Cox bearing an invitation for the Attorney General.

Seated with Kennedy in the ornate paneled rectangle that is the office of the Attorney General, Cox explained his mission. It was this: The University of Georgia had been desegregated for the first time in its history in January, 1961, when Charlayne Hunter and Hamilton Holmes were admitted as students. There had been an initial unsuccessful attempt at violence. Since then the University had reflected in miniature the bitter racial unrest that is endemic to the South. The faculty, the student body and the alumni were gravely concerned over the desegregation problem. Would the Attorney General help them all to find their way by addressing Law Day exercises on May 6?

Kennedy listened to young Cox, questioned him and finally suggested that he clear the invitation formally with the dean of his law school. The new Attorney General was besieged from all sections of the nation with invitations to speak. He had accepted none.

For sheer dramatic impact, no other forum was quite so right for Robert Kennedy's first official enunciation of policy and especially civil rights policy—as the storm-tossed campus in the Deep South state that gave John F. Kennedy his biggest percentage majority in the 1960 presidential election. He accepted the invitation of the college student from Georgia.

When Kennedy went to Athens, Georgia, on May 6, 1961, to speak out on human liberty and the law he did so from a complex and sometimes contradictory background.

It was obvious from the day of his appointment as

Attorney General that civil rights was the big issue hanging over Robert Kennedy's young head.

There had in the beginning been rumblings from the proud legal fraternity against a lawyer without a single day of courtroom experience assuming the office of America's number-one lawyer. This attack never really got off the ground, however, as was shown by the fact that only one member of the United States Senate—Gordon Allott—regarded it as serious enough to vote against Kennedy's confirmation.

Senator Thomas Dodd, a basically conservative Connecticut Democrat, former FBI agent, and distinguished lawyer who helped prosecute Nazi war criminals at Nuremberg, eloquently dismissed the assault on Kennedy's lack of courtroom experience during the Judiciary Committee's confirmation hearing.

Dodd, white-haired and articulate, declared: "Somehow or other, the idea seems to have grown up that the only good lawyer is the successful private practitioner. I do not think this is necessarily so at all. I think all of us who have practiced law privately and served in public office in a legal capacity know this is not true. Some of the finest legal minds are in law schools. Many of them have never privately practiced law. Some of them have been great judges. And I think it is just as true in the case of an Attorney General. I do not accept it as being a fact of life at all that to be an excellent Attorney General one must have made money practicing law."

Aside from the unusual reliance the President placed in him, Robert Kennedy's strongest qualification for the Attorney Generalship was his reputation as a relentless fighter against crime and corruption, whether perpetrated by the underworld, wayward bosses of the labor movement or greedy captains of business and industry. He had pledged to fight these evils with "full

"The happiest family I ever met"—that was the description given Robert and Ethel Kennedy and their seven children by Jacques Lowe, the photographer. The girls, left to right, are Kathleen, 11; Mary Kerry, 3; and Mary Courtney, 7. The boys are, Robert, Jr., 8; David, 7; Michael, 4; and Joseph, 9.

Photographs © Jacques Lowe

Life with Robert Kennedy at McLean, Virginia, and Hyannis Port, Massachusetts, is much as it was in the residences of Joseph P. Kennedy when Robert was growing up with three brothers and five sisters—robust, competitive, noisy. Robert Kennedy has patterned it this way. When touch football is played at Hickory Hill, in McLean, Virginia (above), all members of the family participate and have the privilege of calling signals, as Kathleen is doing (left). At Hyannis Port (right), the Attorney General indulges in a bout of jousting.

Robert Kennedy is a devoted father, athletic competitor, and stern disciplinarian for his youngsters. Although demanding, he can console them, as he is doing with David (left). Above, he rides with Kathleen, who is becoming an adept horsewoman, and below he and Ethel romp with four of the brood.

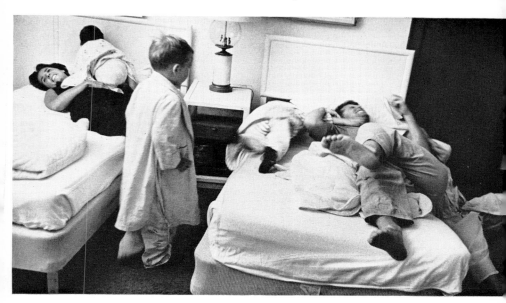

One of the most remarkable of American families is the one reared by Rose and Joseph Kennedy. By their father, Robert Kennedy and his siblings were taught to be tough and competitive. By their mother, they were taught to have deep religious faith. In his complex personality, Robert Kennedy reflects the teachings of both parents. The family portrait (above) groups, in the first row, Patricia, Edward (Teddy), Kathleen, Eunice, and Rosemary. In the back row, are John, Jean, and Robert. Joe, Jr., is absent from the photograph. At the tennis net (below) are Eunice, Bobby, Teddy, and Jean.

Moments of Jubilation. The Brothers Kennedy—Teddy, John and Robert are shown, above, as they arrived for a Washington dinner in 1958, the year John was reelected to the Senate. The photograph below was taken at Hyannis Port the day after John Kennedy was elected President in 1960. Seated are Mrs. A. Sargent Shriver (Eunice Kennedy), Mrs. Joseph P. Kennedy, Joseph P. Kennedy, Mrs. John F. Kennedy, and Teddy Kennedy. Standing are Mrs. Robert Kennedy, Stephen Smith, Mrs. Stephen Smith (Jean Kennedy), President Kennedy, Robert Kennedy, Mrs. Peter Lawford (Patricia Kennedy), R. Sargent Shriver, Mrs. Teddy Kennedy, and Peter Lawford.

Robert Kennedy has stalked Jimmy Hoffa since the two first clashed before the

Senate Rackets Committee in 1957. This confrontation (above) occurred in 1959.

When Robert Kennedy arrived in Los Angeles weeks before the 1960 Democratic National Convention opened, he was confident that his brother would win the Presidential nomination. He worked ceaselessly from a room in the Biltmore Hotel and on the floor of the convention itself (left) to assure the nomination of his brother on the first ballot—a feat the Kennedys accomplished. Robert also played a major role in John Kennedy's decision to offer the Vice-Presidential nomination to Senator Lyndon Johnson of Texas (right). When the Kennedy-Johnson ticket finally won in November, John Kennedy named his brother as Attorney General, but only after Robert Kennedy had spent many weeks pondering the offer.

Wide World

Robert Kennedy often grabs a quick bite at his desk (above). In the summer of 1961, he stood behind the President's desk (right) as John Kennedy signed legislation giving the Attorney General broad powers to fight crime.

vigor" and few questioned his determination to do so.

Kennedy likewise pledged in a colloquy with Senator Estes Kefauver of Tennessee, himself a persistent and successful buster of rackets and trusts, to concentrate on enforcement of the antitrust laws. He told Kefauver he would ferret out and prosecute those who attempted to restrain trade or kill off competition.

As the father of seven children, Kennedy also had a great personal interest in the war against juvenile delinquency. Shortly after the New Frontier took over the reins of government, he and his long-time friend and assistant, David Hackett, took off for New York City to tramp the streets where delinquency has become almost an accepted way of life for those of minority birth who live in squalor and poverty. President Kennedy launched a nationwide drive to stamp out juvenile delinquency soon after that tour and placed the Attorney General and Dave Hackett at its helm.

Civil rights remained. It may seem incongruous that a cosmopolitan son of abolitionist New England, one whose brother had been overwhelmingly triumphant as a vote-getter in the big melting-pot cities of the North, should stand in question on this issue. Yet, because his government service had been as an investigator of crime rather than as a holder of elective office, Robert Kennedy had not filled the public record with his views on racial intolerance and the legal and moral wrongs that spring from it.

Among the more advanced proponents of civil rights action he was also suspect on certain counts. He was the son whom Joseph P. Kennedy described proudly as "most like me." He had been a protégé of Senator John McClellan of Arkansas, a stern defender of the traditions of the Old South. He had shared a warm friendship with the late Senator Joseph McCarthy of Wisconsin, the most hated figure of the era among liberals and a man who savagely trampled the rights of others. There had been protests by members of the American Civil Liberties Union that as chief counsel for the Senate Rackets Committee Kennedy had not been zealous enough in protecting the rights of witnesses.

It was Robert Kennedy who gave the signal from the Kennedy camp that led to the drafting of a powerful civil rights platform at the Democratic national convention in Los Angeles in 1960. Yet this could be written off as political expediency, as a necessity if John Kennedy were to capture his party's presidential nomination.

Senator Kenneth Keating, a witty and astute Republican from New York, sought a firm civil rights commitment from Robert Kennedy during the latter's Senate confirmation hearing.

Kennedy stated his position in these words: "My general philosophy is that we have to move strongly and vigorously in the field of civil rights. I do not think that this is a subject or matter that can be solved overnight, however. I think that there has to be an understanding and tolerance on all sides."

Keating, one of the Senate's most vocal advocates of broader Federal authority to wipe out racial discrimination and segregation, pursued his point. In keeping with the eloquent Democratic platform which Kennedy supported, would the Attorney General seek such authority in new legislation?

Kennedy refused to be pinned down to specific proposals. He stated only that he would await "my instructions and guidance from President-elect Kennedy."

Four Democratic Senators from the Deep South— McClellan, Jim Eastland of Mississippi, Olin Johnston of South Carolina, and Sam Ervin of North Carolina—

also sat on the Judiciary Committee that day, January 13, 1961. All had denounced the Supreme Court's 1954 school desegregation ruling with vehemence and regularity. All had fought with parliamentary skill and oratorical flamboyance to prevent passage of civil rights legislation.

Not one of the four questioned Robert Kennedy on any phase of the civil rights question during that hearing. They failed even to ask if and how he planned to enforce public school integration.

It must be explained, of course, that Southerners who have made their way to the United States Senate and remained there for a number of years are, with but two or three exceptions, realistic and philosophical individuals. When the chips are down, they practice party loyalty and regularity. They realize also that for all their political plastering and patching, the façade of Old Dixie is crumbling. Their job merely is to hold it together as long as possible.

This purpose could not be served by antagonizing a new Attorney General for whom they had warm personal regard and who happened to be the brother of the President of the United States.

Eastland, chairman of the committee and a national symbol of the South's fanatical struggle to retain white supremacy and racial segregation, introduced Robert Kennedy's nomination on the Senate floor on January 21 and led off the plaudits. The Mississippian told his colleagues that young Kennedy "has a fine legal mind, he is sincere, his personal life is clean; and it is the judgment of the committee that he is qualified in every respect for his appointment."

Then came McClellan, a man whose life has been stalked by tragedy. When the last of his three sons died in an airplane crash at the height of the Rackets Committee probe, McClellan flew home to Little Rock with

Robert Kennedy at his side. The Senator was lost and in the words of one person close to the scene at the time "wanted to give up everything."

But Kennedy, who knew the meaning of personal tragedy from the untimely deaths of his brother Joe and his sister Kathleen, was a source of tremendous strength to McClellan. In some ways he practically became McClellan's fourth son.

On the Senate floor McClellan spoke with fatherly pride of the young man who had worked at his side for seven years. He recalled the job Bob had done for him on the Rackets Committee. "As an organizer, coordinator, supervisor and director, the Honorable Robert F. Kennedy demonstrated beyond question superb qualities of both administration and executive leadership," declared McClellan. "He demonstrated professional ability which convinced me beyond all doubt that he is capable of making a great Attorney General."

As other Southerners echoed McClellan's praise, Dixie made a strong case for the thirty-five-year-old Irish Catholic from Massachusetts to be Attorney General.

Southern support was not, however, the genesis of all doubts about Robert Kennedy's devotion to civil rights and other causes associated with political liberalism. The roots of distrust actually ran back into the activities and outspoken statements of Joseph P. Kennedy over a period of nearly thirty years.

Probably no other member of Franklin D. Roosevelt's New Deal was looked upon with as much suspicion by staunch liberals as the elder Kennedy. Among the men and women who helped Roosevelt execute his social and economic revolution within the American government, Joseph P. Kennedy was regarded by many as a clever money man from Boston whose interest in reform began and ended with protection of the dollar and the means of making it. Yet even those who distrusted him could not but be awed by his amazing ability to get a job done with a minimum of talk and time. Roosevelt himself found Kennedy a brilliant administrator and a delightful companion.

Joseph Kennedy is a shrewd, skillful and sometimes ruthless financier and business operator who has accumulated a fortune estimated in excess of two hundred million dollars. He possesses a devotion to his immediate family that long-time visitors to the Kennedy homes at Hyannisport and Palm Beach describe as magnificent and fanatical. In a life of accomplishment that would make even Horatio Alger appear a pallid American hero, Joseph Kennedy also has numbered some of the most powerful men in the world among both his friends and enemies.

One former Democratic senator, who served with Kennedy in the Roosevelt Administration and shared his isolationist views, bluntly states that in the era of the 1930's when a strong sense of social consciousness guided most government officials: "Joe Kennedy was merely interested in making money."

Such a characterization sells Joe Kennedy far short. It does not take into account the fact that he was vitally interested in the preservation of a strong government during a period of financial chaos and that he supported much of what Roosevelt was attempting to do —and wrote a book, *I'm for Roosevelt,* in 1936 to prove it. Nor does such a characterization take note of the Kennedy-donated hospital, educational and church facilities around the nation that attest his generosity.

But had Joe Kennedy been the most avid social reformer of them all, the sin that many liberals could never forgive was his outspoken isolationism in the years when the United States was moving toward war with Adolf Hitler and his Axis associates in Italy and Japan.

It has become popular in recent years to claim that liberal and conservative labels have no meaning in the area of foreign policy. One basis for this contention is that the great progressives of the first four decades of the twentieth century—men of the gigantic stature of William Borah of Idaho, Burton K. Wheeler of Montana, Hiram Johnson of California—formed the hard core of isolationist opposition in Congress to Roosevelt's steps toward involvement in war. Yet there were millions of Americans who regarded themselves as progressives or liberals or New Dealers who stood with Roosevelt on the war issue as they had on domestic reform and actually provided the broad basis of popular support needed by the President to advance his program of aid to Great Britain and other victims of Hitlerian aggression. Most of these Americans felt a strong sense of personal involvement in the conflict, not alone because Hitler had overrun less powerful nations but also because he was one of history's bloodiest bigots, a man who committed mass murders for reasons of race and religion. They could not divorce the battle against Hitler from the battle to preserve the rights of man.

Joseph P. Kennedy, as Ambassador to the Court of St. James, saw the conflict from a different vantage point. He was highly disturbed by the political situation within Great Britain. And he feared that involvement of the United States in the fight between England and Germany posed a lethal danger to his country.

In October, 1940, Kennedy returned home from his ambassadorial post to publicly support Roosevelt for a third term. But it already was apparent that his views of the world situation were at such variance with those of the President that his tenure in London was ended.

Shortly after Roosevelt won re-election, Kennedy handed in his resignation and the President gladly accepted it.

Once he was free of an official post in the Roosevelt Administration, Joe Kennedy pursued the cause of anti-involvement more vehemently. As late as the spring of 1941, when events were catapulting America swiftly toward armed intervention, he was warning America: "This country must not become a belligerent just because we love Churchill and hate Hitler. We cannot divert the tides of mighty revolution now sweeping Asia and Europe. An attempt to do so would end in failure and disgrace abroad, in disillusionment and bankruptcy at home."

During this period Robert Kennedy was the only one of Joe's sons living at home with his family who was old enough to understand his father's ordeal. Joe and John were away at college. Edward was too young to realize the implications of the war in Europe.

Robert recalls that he shared his father's feelings against involvement in war, but adds: "I don't remember that anyone asked my views."

Again, ten years later, when America under President Truman was struggling to build the North Atlantic Alliance into a strong military unit in the face of Soviet aggression, Joe Kennedy joined former President Hoover and the late Senator Robert A. Taft in opposing involvement in Europe's affairs.

One of the highest hurdles John Kennedy had to surmount in his quest for the Democratic presidential nomination was the belief held by liberal Democrats that he was Joe Kennedy's son in thought and deed as well as by birth.

Truman confided privately to friends that he regarded John Kennedy as an able and intelligent young man who would acquit himself well in any job.

But, said the former President, he shuddered at the thought of "Joe Kennedy in the White House."

In a nationally televised attempt to block Jack's nomination, Truman made the Freudian slip of referring to the presidential aspirant as Joseph Kennedy. Mrs. Eleanor Roosevelt's opposition to John Kennedy likewise sprang in part from her fear that Joe Kennedy would influence his son's approach to public policy.

So great was the antagonism toward Joe Kennedy within the liberal wing of the Democratic party that John Kennedy did not make a single public appearance with his father until the day after the election.

Since Joseph P. Kennedy is a ruggedly independent soul who has carved a fabulous, productive life according to the dictates of his own will and conscience rather than the whims of public opinion, he has not been greatly concerned about his Madison Avenue image. He is not a man to change his course with each new zephyr of popular sentiment. He, therefore, is a man about whom there are many misconceptions and apprehensions. Since Robert Kennedy shares many of the personality and character traits of his father, some of these misconceptions and apprehensions followed him into the Attorney Generalship. He was particularly suspect among very avid champions of civil rights who questioned his dedication to the cause of racial equality. The Attorney General is inclined to drift off into a nebulous answer when asked if his actions in the area of civil rights have been influenced by this skepticism.

Yet he literally poured his heart and his mind into the speech he took with him to Athens, Georgia, on May 6, 1961, putting it through at least a half dozen drafts before hitting upon a final product that stated properly his personal views and those of John Kennedy's administration on civil rights.

When Robert Kennedy arrived at the University of Georgia, he stepped into a tense situation. Prior to his arrival a band of pickets marched through the campus carrying *Yankee Go Home* signs. There had been minor incidents the previous evening in protest against his appearance in Georgia.

The performance the Attorney General gave before a critical, highly educated audience of 1,600 Georgians was probably his best on a public platform up to that time. He was sober, self-assured, emphatic. His suit as usual was a conservative dark blue. The famed unruly shock of sandy hair was combed neatly into place.

The Georgia address, excerpts of which later were run on nationwide television, was especially impressive to those who recalled Kennedy's first miserable attempt at public speaking in 1955. On that occasion, he described, with the aid of slides, the trip he had taken through Central Asia with Associate Justice William O. Douglas.

Lem Billings, a family friend who has known Kennedy since he was "a nice little boy" at Hyannisport, recalls that he worked "very hard" preparing the 1955 speech, but had a "very difficult time" delivering it. Angela Novello, Bob's personal secretary for a half dozen years, likewise remembers that "he was very hesitant in his speech and just wasn't good."

There was no trace of the shy, fumbling Kennedy of yesteryear in the forceful young Attorney General who addressed the University of Georgia. Facing an audience that certainly included bitter antagonists, in a region where politicians and demagogues had preached disobedience to Federal law, Kennedy declared that man cannot live without law to tell him what is right and what is wrong, what is permitted and what is prohibited.

Kennedy said: "We know that it is law which enables men to live together, that creates order out of chaos. We know that law is the glue that holds civilization together.

"And we know that if one man's rights are denied, the rights of all are endangered. In our country the courts have a most important role in safeguarding these rights. The decisions of the courts, however much we might disagree with them, in the final analysis must be followed and respected. If we disagree with a court decision and, thereafter, irresponsibly assail the court and defy its rulings, we challenge the foundations of our society."

In light of the growing communist challenge and the recent ill-starred Cuban invasion, the Attorney General stated that "the time has long since passed when the people of the United States can be apathetic about their belief and respect for the law and about the necessity of placing our own house in order.... As we turn to meet our enemy, to look him full in the face," said Kennedy, "we cannot afford feet of clay or an arm of glass."

He turned then to the "three areas of difficulty within the purview of my responsibilities that sap our national strength, that weaken our people, that require our immediate attention." These three areas, of course, were organized crime, business monopoly and civil rights.

Of the first, Kennedy said: "In too many major communities of our country, organized crime has become big business. It knows no state lines. It drains off millions of dollars of our national wealth, infecting legitimate businesses, labor unions and even sports. Tolerating organized crime promotes the cheap philosophy that everything is a racket. It promotes cynicism among adults. It contributes to the confusion of the young and to the increase of juvenile delinquency.

"It is not the gangster himself who is of concern. It is what he is doing to our cities, our communities, our moral fiber. Ninety per cent of the major racketeers would be out of business by the end of this year if the ordinary citizen, the businessman, the union official and the public authority stood up to be counted and refused to be corrupted . . . unless the basic attitude changes here in this country, the rackets will prosper and grow."

Although he is the son of a giant of the business world, Robert Kennedy during his days as chief counsel for the Senate Rackets Committee had been as tough on the fast-buck, double-dealing boys of management as on the Hoffas, Becks and Crosses who prostituted their leadership of the union movement. In Athens, Georgia, he made it clear that his attitude would be the same now that he was Attorney General.

He lashed out at the so-called "respectables" of the business community who were responsible for a nationwide spread of price-fixing and contended that their activities were "merely symptomatic of many other practices commonly accepted in business life."

"Our enemies assert that capitalism enslaves the worker and will destroy itself," said Kennedy. "It is our national faith that the system of competitive enterprise offers the best hope for individual freedom, social development and economic growth. Thus, every businessman who cheats on his taxes, fixes prices or underpays his labor, every union official who makes a collusive deal or misuses union funds, damages the free enterprise system in the eyes of the world and does a disservice to the millions of honest Americans in all walks of life."

Kennedy finally arrived at the subject his audience awaited, the one which he said "affects us all the most directly—civil rights."

Millions of words are spoken or shouted or whispered each year in America on this most basic human matter that has divided the United States for more than a century. The words emanate from the pulpit, the halls of Congress, the political forum, the state legislature, the civic club or from a hoarse and ugly voice in a howling mob. Seldom have the words been more candid or penetrating than those spoken by Robert F. Kennedy in segregated Georgia. He viewed the struggle of blacks to attain equality with whites not simply as one that had to be solved because United States law and domestic politics so dictated, but one that had to be solved because it was part of a dynamic grass-roots stirring in the world that could determine ultimately whether democracy or communism prevails on earth.

The Attorney General declared: "First let me say this: the time has long since arrived when loyal Americans must measure the impact of their actions beyond the limits of their own towns or states. For instance, we must be quite aware of the fact that fifty per cent of the countries in the United Nations are not white; that around the world, in Africa, South America and Asia, people whose skins are a different color than ours are on the move to gain their measure of freedom and liberty.

"From the Congo to Cuba, from South Vietnam to Algiers, in India, Brazil and Iran, men and women and children are straightening their backs and listening— to the evil promises of communist tyranny and the honorable promises of Anglo-American liberty. And those people will decide not only their future but how the cause of freedom fares in the world. . . . In the worldwide struggle, the graduation at this University of Charlayne Hunter and Hamilton Holmes will without question aid and assist the fight against communist political infiltration and guerrilla warfare. . . . When parents send their children to school this fall in Atlanta, peaceably and in accordance with the rule of law, barefoot Burmese and Congolese will see before their eyes Americans living by the rule of law."

Ten days earlier Kennedy had intervened to open public schools in Prince Edward County, Virginia, where 1,700 Negro children had had no schooling for nearly two years and 1,400 white children had attended private schools financed by state funds.

The Attorney General explained his action to his Georgia audience. He also spoke with feeling about the ordeal the South had been suffering as a result of the Supreme Court's school desegregation order—a decision that "required action of the most difficult, delicate and complex nature, going to the heart of Southern institutions." He said he had intervened in Prince Edward County to maintain the order of the court as his oath required. But Kennedy was firm about where he stood.

"In this case—in all cases—I say to you today that if the orders of the court are circumvented, the Department of Justice will act.

"We will not stand by or be aloof. We will move!"

He continued: "I happen to believe that the 1954 decision was right. But my belief does not matter—it is the law. Some of you may believe the decision was wrong. That does not matter. It is the law. And we both respect the law. By facing this problem honorably, you have shown to all the world that we Americans are moving forward together—solving this problem— under the rule of law. . . . My firm belief is that if we are to make progress in this area—if we are to be truly great as a nation, then we must make sure that nobody is denied an opportunity because of race, creed or color. . . . For on this generation of Americans falls the full burden of proving to the world that we really mean it when we say all men are created free and are equal before the law. . . .

"You may ask, will we enforce the Civil Rights statutes.

"The answer is: 'Yes, we will.' "

Kennedy ended his speech by quoting the words spoken by a famed Georgian, Henry W. Grady, in Massachusetts in 1889: "A mighty duty, sir, a mighty inspiration impels everyone of us tonight to lose in patriotic consecration whatever estranges, whatever divides. We, sir, are Americans—and we stand for human liberty!"

Some Southern newspapers castigated the Attorney General for upholding the Supreme Court decision. Others praised the candor of his approach.

On the wall of a small room that is part of the Attorney General's sprawling fifth-floor office suite in the Department of Justice hangs a map of the United States punctured by as many as one hundred brightly colored pins.

Kennedy is proud of what those pins stand for: individual investigations of charges that Negroes have been denied their vote in communities of the South. The pins cover most of the Southern area of the map but are most heavily concentrated in Alabama, Mississippi and northern Louisiana.

To Bob Kennedy, this is the way out for the Negro. He is critical of what he regards as the inertia of his predecessor, William Rogers, on the civil rights issue and especially in the area of voting rights.

"The long-range solution for Negroes is voting rights," says Kennedy. "I think all other rights for which they are fighting will flow from that. Political power comes from votes and rights come from political power."

But, he emphasizes, Negroes must help themselves. They must attempt to register and to vote.

"Negroes can get the vote in the South in the foreseeable future—if they do something," explains the Cabinet officer charged with enforcement of the Federal voting rights statute. "But there are a lot of counties where they never have attempted to register."

It is the Attorney General's conviction that once the Negro begins to make himself felt in the polling place, the old-line Southern politician who stands only for white supremacy and segregation will begin to fade from the land. Kennedy does not rule out the possible need for additional legislation in the civil rights field. But in his first year in the Cabinet he was not ready to seek such legislation.

The President's brother is of the opinion, however, that the New Frontier in its first year provided Negroes in all sections of the nation with some very substantial gains that civil rights legislation could not give them. These were the gains that stemmed from an increased and expanded national minimum wage, a liberalized Social Security law, broad and generous new housing legislation, improved unemployment benefits and assistance for dependent children. He saw additional benefits for Negroes in two measures the President proposed but failed to attain—Federal aid to education and medical insurance for the aged.

At the end of the first session of the 87th Congress, Attorney General Kennedy said the Negro had profited more from the passage of a broad spectrum of social and economic legislation than he would have had Congress become embroiled in a bitter dispute over civil rights that might have armed the Federal Government with greater authority to enforce integration but also would have intensified the hatred between the races.

This Kennedy concept is in the Roosevelt tradition.

The New Deal President was not successful in attaining congressional action in the civil rights field, but his vast reforms did raise the working and living standards of Negroes far above those of the impoverished past and they did give Negroes a dignity they had not previously been able to attain in the American community. These were the basic bread-and-status reasons why Negroes broke with their Republican tradition in the 1930's and became a most powerful ingredient in that strange, colorful political concoction of majorities and minorities called the Democratic party. These also were the reasons why a preponderence of Negroes voted for John Kennedy over Richard Nixon in 1960, although Nixon's basic civil rights record as congressman, Senator and Vice President was more impressive than Kennedy's.

There is without doubt some political motivation in Robert Kennedy's approach to the tragic racial dispute that makes an angry dichotomy of the world's mightiest nation at the time of its greatest crisis. He could not act without some political concern, for he is a Cabinet member in a Democratic administration, the brother of a president who will seek a second term in 1964, and enough of a pragmatist to know that you cannot get the job done in public life unless you can get elected.

But Robert Kennedy's doctrine runs deeper than this. He possesses a conviction, based upon both his religious and legal training, that all men stand equal before God and the Law. He also is an introspective and independent-minded human being who honestly believes he has an understanding of the position of the Reverend Martin Luther King on one side and of Senator John McClellan on the other.

"Exercising my responsibilities as Attorney General of the United States," he says, "I'm going to cross somebody. Maybe one day it's going to be Martin Luther King and maybe one day it's going to be John Patterson. I don't want the Department of Justice to be owned by any organization. The NAACP is not making decisions here, nor is any group. And they know it!"

They do indeed know it and both sides have sounded their protests—in public, in print, at the White House, in the Attorney General's private chambers. They knew it five months after the New Frontier took over the Washington scene. For exactly two weeks after Robert Kennedy made his declaration in Athens—"We will not stand by or be aloof. We will move"—his words were being subjected to the full test and fury of the challenge they laid down. The cherry trees were safe. Robert Kennedy had to prove that the tree of liberty also was safe.

Chapter Eight
All Necessary Steps

ABOUT TWO O'CLOCK ON THE MORNING OF MAY 22, 1961, Robert Kennedy stood at the high window directly behind his desk in the Department of Justice, staring down into the dark, silent emptiness of Constitution Avenue and on to the dingy gray façade of the Natural History Museum across the street. His slight, shirt-sleeved figure appeared elflike, framed as it was by voluminous folds of red and beige draperies that hung from ceiling to floor.

Suddenly the young Attorney General swung around,

clenched his fingers into the back of his red leather chair and, to two associates standing across the desk, declared: "Those people are scared—and I don't blame them!"

Moments earlier, before turning to gaze out into the warm spring night, Kennedy had talked by telephone with the Reverend Martin Luther King, huddled with his prayerful, hymn-singing brood of Freedom Riders inside the besieged First Baptist Church of Montgomery, Alabama. Outside the church, a violent mob of white Southerners demanded the blood of those who dared break their rigid rules against integrated public transportation and were intent upon drawing it.

Only 150 Federal law-enforcement officers, rushed to Montgomery by the Attorney General, stood between King's congregation and death.

This was Robert Kennedy's baptism of fire as the chief law-enforcement officer of the United States. He stood—a worried, determined young man—amid the flames of the nation's most divisive and continuing domestic problem, armed by President Kennedy with almost unlimited authority to handle the grave situation.

The Attorney General felt compassion and responsibility for the Freedom Riders sent into the angry South by the Congress of Racial Equality (CORE) to change a way of life that has existed for more than a century. But he was explicit in stating that he considered their attempt to break the racial barrier in this manner ill-advised. "They should be using this energy and talent and initiative to register their votes," Kennedy said as he went about the difficult task of protecting their lives and upholding their legal right to ride unsegregated on public vehicles.

Kennedy also had an understanding of the terrible dilemma facing the South in a period of social and political upheaval. Yet he had made it clear to Southern leaders that he would act swiftly and boldly to halt all attempts to circumvent Federal law. This law included a ruling by the United States Supreme Court in December, 1960, that interstate passengers have a right to service "without discrimination."

It would be difficult to determine where the road to Montgomery's mob violence actually began. It certainly was winding its way through the South long before the Freedom Riders arrived in Alabama's capital city.

For Robert Kennedy one phase of the saga began in 1958, when he still was chief counsel for the Senate Rackets Committee and John Kennedy was the junior Senator from Massachusetts, intent upon winning reelection that year and upon capturing the Democratic presidential nomination two years hence.

Robert Kennedy went to Alabama in 1958 to make a speech about his sensational investigation of corruption and gangsterism in the union-management field and there met John Patterson. Patterson, then only thirty-seven years old, was somewhat in the mold of Kennedy himself. He had been an outstanding racket-busting state Attorney General and had just been elected Governor.

The young Senate investigator and the young Governor were impressed with each other; so much so that Patterson invited Kennedy to address the State Legislature. Kennedy had to decline the invitation because of a prior commitment in Washington, but in Patterson he had found an able political ally.

"We got along very well," says Kennedy, looking back at his first meeting with Patterson.

Shortly after these two men met in Alabama, Patterson and Jack Kennedy got together. The result was that Patterson became a stalwart in the preconvention fight then being launched by the Kennedys.

"Patterson was our first break in the Solid South," says Robert.

Despite heavy pressures on the Governor to back the candidacy of Senator Lyndon B. Johnson of Texas, he stuck with Kennedy. After Kennedy had been nominated for President and Johnson for Vice President, Patterson continued to play an important part in the Kennedy political operation.

"He was very interested in getting my brother elected," explains Robert Kennedy. "He worked hard, under difficult circumstances."

A strong personal and political bond thus bound Patterson and the Kennedys as a first group of militant young Freedom Riders, members of CORE, entered Alabama from Georgia on Mother's Day, May 14, 1961.

Starting from Washington, D.C., on May 4, to challenge with Ghandi-like nonviolence "every form of segregation met by the bus passenger," the group of six whites and seven Negroes traveled in peace through Virginia, North Carolina and Georgia. The only real skirmish they faced prior to their entry into Alabama was a roughing up of three Riders at the Greyhound bus terminal in Rock Hill, South Carolina, on May 9.

As the Riders began their journey from Atlanta into Alabama on Mother's Day, they divided themselves into two groups—one traveling by Greyhound bus, the other by Trailways bus. Up to this moment the Attorney General was not even aware of their mission through the Southland. But two of his top assistants, Assistant Attorney General Burke Marshall and Edwin O. Guthman, Kennedy's public information officer, had read an April 26 announcement by James Farmer, National Director of CORE, of the Riders' intentions to travel from Washington to New Orleans. They watched the Riders' progress from afar, but had little reason to expect violence in Alabama after the integrated group had ridden in relative serenity through four other Confederate states.

On the night of Sunday, May 14, however, the Greyhound bus was attacked in Anniston, Alabama, by a crowd wielding clubs, chains, and blackjacks. The vehicle finally was stalled six miles east of Anniston and burned by a fire bomb. A number of the Riders were injured. The Trailways bus got through to Birmingham, but there its passengers were beaten up when they stepped off of it. Despite warnings from the FBI to the Birmingham police that violence could be expected, there were no police at the terminal to protect the passengers. They arrived ten minutes after the violence erupted. The reason given for the delay by the police chief was that he was shorthanded because it was Mother's Day.

When news of the two incidents reached Washington on the morning of Monday, May 15, Deputy Attorney General Byron White telephoned Kennedy to report the violence in Alabama and to ask his guidance.

"He told me he thought we ought to make preparations," says White. "He agreed there was enough indication of trouble down there that we ought to be prepared."

The immediate task facing Kennedy and White, however, was to get the Freedom Riders out of Birmingham. Because mob rule already had begun to prevail in Alabama, there was not a Greyhound bus driver in that city who was willing to man a vehicle carrying the Riders.

The Attorney General decided it was time to have a man of his own on the scene to report exactly what was happening and to act as intermediary, if one was needed, with either or both elements in the bitter controversy. The obvious choice from his personal standpoint was his administrative assistant, John Seigenthaler, himself a Southerner and former newspaper reporter who exposed flagrant Teamsters Union hoodlumism for the *Nashville Tennessean.*

Kennedy also summoned into the foray a close political friend of Governor Patterson's, Charles Merriweather, who was in the South at the time. Merriweather, who had just won a blistering Senate fight over his nomination by President Kennedy to serve on the Board of Directors of the Export-Import Bank, at first resisted the Attorney General's suggestion that he attempt to persuade Patterson to protect the Freedom Riders.

When Merriweather demanded to know what the Freedom Riders were doing in his segregated state, Kennedy replied: "It's not a question of what they're doing. It's a question of their right to travel."

Kennedy pointed out that the Freedom Riders were determined to get through to New Orleans. "If they don't make it," he told Merriweather, "if they are forced to return to New York, there'll be others."

Merriweather agreed to act as go-between for the Attorney General with Patterson, but was unable to locate the Governor. At the same time Seigenthaler was on his way to Birmingham.

Kennedy, meanwhile, had established contact with Floyd Mann, Alabama's Commissioner of Public Safety, and Mann obtained assurances from Patterson that the Freedom Riders would be given protection to travel the ninety miles from Birmingham to Montgomery. Mann asked Kennedy whether the Riders themselves would be willing to "get on a bus and get out of there."

To learn the answer to this question, the Attorney General talked by telephone with a leader of the Riders. This representative of the Riders could not commit his fellow segregation-breakers without consulting them. But a half hour later he telephoned the Attorney General to state that they would be willing to travel by bus under police protection.

"I asked them if they would go on the first bus available and they said they would," says Kennedy.

But fifteen minutes later Mann called the Attorney General to report: "We've got the police protection but now the bus-company drivers won't drive the bus and the company says they can't obtain drivers." Mann, who was working closely with Kennedy, also told the Attorney General that crowds were gathering at the bus terminal and that "a very serious situation" was developing.

Kennedy and Mann agreed that it would be wise for the Attorney General himself to call an official of the bus company, and Mann suggested that he talk with George E. Cruit, superintendent of the Greyhound terminal in Birmingham.

In an interview with *U. S. News and World Report* in October, 1961, Kennedy explained his purpose for calling Cruit in these words: "So I called Mr. Cruit—for the sole purpose of working with the State authorities and to insure that no one would be beaten or killed.

"This was not a case of the Federal Government coming in and stirring up trouble. I never even knew the 'Freedom Riders' were going to Alabama until I read in the morning paper that this group was in Birmingham. Everything that was done by us was done with the full knowledge and concurrence of the State authorities."

On the telephone with Kennedy on the afternoon of May 15, Cruit contended that every one of his drivers was fearful for his life and refused to drive an integrated bus. While Cruit and the Attorney General sparred over the long-distance line, Cruit's secretary took down the conversation.

According to her notes, after Cruit said he could not find a single union driver to take the Freedom Riders out of Birmingham, Kennedy declared: "Mr. Cruit, I think if I were you I would get a driver of one of the colored buses and have them take the bus down. You can get one of them, can't you?"

"No," replied Cruit.

"Well, hell, you can look for one, can't you?" exploded the Attorney General. "After all, these people have tickets and are entitled to transportation to continue the trip or project to Montgomery. We have gone to a lot of trouble to see that they get to this trip and I am most concerned to see that it is accomplished."

These words were picked up by newspapers throughout the South—printed and reprinted—as proof positive that the President's brother deliberately sent a mixed racial group into Dixie to crack the segregation laws. They were utilized by Governor Patterson in a tirade against the Attorney General.

Not only does Kennedy deny having any hand in the trip of the Freedom Riders, but his associates point out he was far too busy working on a survey of United States intelligence activities in the wake of the tragic attempt by anti-Castro Cubans to invade their homeland to know that the Riders were on the move in Dixie.

In his conversation with Cruit, Kennedy finally suggested that the Greyhound superintendent himself drive the Freedom Riders to Montgomery. Cruit replied that he did not know how.

The exasperated Attorney General barked: "Well, surely somebody in the damn bus company can drive a bus, can't they?"

Cruit protested that he and his fellow executives were in the "administrative end" of the business. He also explained that "a bus costs $45,000 and amateurs can't handle them."

Kennedy, incensed by Cruit's claim that there was not a single person in a city of 355,000 who would drive the Freedom Riders to Montgomery, told the supervisor to get in touch "with Mr. Greyhound or whoever Greyhound is and somebody better give us an answer to this question."

"I am—the Government is—going to be very much upset if the group does not get to continue their trip," said the Attorney General. "In fact, I suggest you make arrangements to get a driver immediately and get these people on the way to Montgomery. Under the law they are entitled to transportation provided by Greyhound and we are looking for you to get them on their way."

Cruit finally agreed that "I shall be glad to do what I can."

In the end, however, though one airplane was grounded by weather and a second because of a bomb threat, the Freedom Riders were flown rather than driven out of Birmingham. They went to New Orleans and immediately were put in police custody. Kennedy sent Seigenthaler along to keep an eye on the situation. On Thursday, May 18, however, a group of college students, who also called themselves Freedom Riders, headed toward Birmingham and Kennedy ordered Seigenthaler back to that troubled community.

By the time the Attorney General's man arrived in Birmingham, the new crop of segregation-breakers was in jail. Eventually Birmingham Police Commissioner Eugene T. (Bull) Connor hustled them back to Tennessee, from whence they had come. But as Connor left, they promised to be back in Birmingham by noon the next day—and they were.

Tension now was mounting swiftly and dangerously all over Alabama. The unrest was spreading into neighboring states. There also were reports that Negro and white college students would be flooding into the state from all sections of the nation as part of the Freedom Riders movement.

The telephone line between the White House and the Justice Department—between the private office of one Kennedy and the private office of another—was frequently busy. The Attorney General and his assistants, acting with the advice and approval of the President, continued to contact Negro and white leaders in both North and South imploring them not to pour fuel on the fire in Alabama.

The Attorney General alerted a group of 20 U. S. Marshals in Washington to be ready to move at any moment. He also tried for two days to reach Governor Patterson by telephone but was told he was not available.

At noon on Friday, May 19, the President also made an attempt to call Patterson and was given the same answer.

The President that day gathered Robert Kennedy, Deputy Attorney General Byron White, and Assistant Attorney General Burke Marshall in his office at the White House to go over the situation in Alabama—to determine what the Federal Government could do and should do. Through John Kennedy's conversation ran one basic contention: The Federal Government must not step in until a "maximum effort" had been made to let local authorities handle the problem.

The elusive John Patterson, meanwhile, had decided that the time had come for him to communicate with Washington. He still was not ready to talk personally with his old political pals, Jack and Bob Kennedy. But he had an intermediary notify the White House that he would be willing to consult with a representative of the President.

The President immediately designated John Seigenthaler, who already was in Birmingham, as his representative. It, of course, was no coincidence that Seigenthaler also happened to be in Alabama as the personal representative of the Attorney General.

Seigenthaler hurried to Montgomery and when he walked into the Governor's office it was as if he had jumped from a plane into a hurricane. Patterson knew that Robert Kennedy had his U. S. Marshals ready to plunge into Alabama to escort the Freedom Riders and he did not like it one bit. Not only did the Governor think the Federal Government had no right to intervene in his sovereign state, he also had an allergy (whose primary manifestation was a raging outburst of temper) to the word "escort."

Seigenthaler pointed out that the President and the Attorney General had the responsibility to uphold Federal law and to prevent interference with interstate transportation.

"We have the manpower, the equipment, the will and the desire to protect all the people in Alabama— whether residents or visitors," retorted Patterson. "We intend to give this protection on the highways and elsewhere. We will give equal protection to all passengers without giving special protection to any."

The angry Governor added: "You can tell that to the press, the Attorney General and the bus officials."

Although Patterson was furious over Kennedy's projected intervention, he gave Seigenthaler the impression that he was in control of the situation in Alabama and there would be no problem. This impression was reported back to the President and the Attorney General. Seigenthaler telephoned his information to the Attorney General while still in Patterson's presence.

When Seigenthaler made his report, Robert Kennedy told him that if Patterson carried through on his pledge to "protect all people in Alabama" he would not send Federal marshals into the state.

At this particular period in the Alabama crisis, Seigenthaler says, the Attorney General's attitude toward Patterson could best be described as "friendly but firm." Patterson promised that the following morning, Saturday, May 20, he would give the Freedom Riders full protection on their bus trip from Birmingham to Montgomery. He said he was opposed to them moving at night because it would be too easy for someone to fire into the bus in the dark.

Patterson fulfilled his promise. The bus carrying the Freedom Riders rolled along the highway from Birmingham to Montgomery with escort and without incident.

Seigenthaler was in Montgomery, ready to watch the arrival of the harassed group and to report what he saw to Kennedy in Washington. With him was John Doar, First Assistant Attorney General in the Civil Rights Division.

As the time approached for the bus to pull into the Montgomery terminal, Seigenthaler and Doar drove down to the station to watch its arrival. They expected the calm of the ninety-mile highway journey to prevail in the capital city.

The two representatives of the U. S. Government drove first to the U. S. Attorney's office, which is about one block from the bus terminal but within good view of it. Doar alighted there. Seigenthaler told him he would drive on down to the terminal to see if the Riders had arrived. He had not progressed half a block when it became sickeningly apparent to him that the small band of young Negroes and whites had arrived ahead of schedule and a bloody race riot was in full swing in the environs of the depot. Doar, from his vantage point in the Federal Building, also saw what was happening.

Seigenthaler decided to drive around the block to get a full view of the proceedings. The view he got was blinding.

First, the former Tennessee newsman with the gentle drawl and quiet manner was appalled to see the luggage of the Freedom Riders being hurled over a wall by white Southerners whose single motivation of the instant was a lust to hurt—and probably to kill.

He watched in horror as a terrified Negro boy ran for his life with a band of violent, jeering men at his heels. He saw the Riders beaten, vilified, and chased by about one hundred fanatical segregationists.

Cruising slowly through this bedlam in his car, Seigenthaler spied a white girl being hounded by seven or eight white men and one vicious white woman as she attempted to flee the terminal. The woman kept slamming a big black handbag into the girl's head and goading the men into harming her. Each time the bag hit, the girl's head thumped to one side like a punching bag.

Seigenthaler decided he had to help the girl. He pulled his car up beside her and jumped out of it. He grabbed at the girl's arm, but she pulled away, crying: "Listen, Mister, go away. Don't get yourself hurt for my sake. This is my fight. Go away. Please leave me alone. Go out of here, Mister!"

Those were the last words the Attorney General's assistant remembers from that grotesque episode. As the girl pulled from his grasp, Seigenthaler was blinded and knocked unconscious by a heavy blow on the head.

For nearly thirty minutes the thirty-three-year-old official who had been designated two days earlier as "the President's personal representative" lay on the sidewalks of the state capital of Alabama.

Finally Seigenthaler was taken to a local hospital, where doctors, nurses and other attendants indicated their shame and embarrassment at the incident. The explanation for the delay in getting him to the hospital was that "all white ambulances" in Montgomery had broken down.

Doar did not witness the Seigenthaler beating. Instead, from an office in the Federal Building, he telephoned the Department of Justice in Washington, got Assistant Attorney General Burke Marshall and Ed Guthman on the line at 12:25 p.m. and began a vivid description of the horrendous drama then being acted out on the street below him.

Because Doar himself was shocked by the spectacle at the bus terminal, his account was a jumble of words and emotions. "It's just terrible ... worst thing I've ever seen ... just terrible ... fists ... thugs ... pushing ... they're bleeding ... it's terrible. ... It's led by a guy with a bleeding face ... when the bus pulled in, two women standing on a corner of the platform yelled, 'There those niggers are' ... the mob came running down the street ... the women yelled 'Get 'em, get 'em' ... there's not a cop in sight ... they're beating them now ... it's terrible."

Guthman immediately notified White, and the Deputy Attorney General decreed that the time for action had arrived. He was not authorized to take it, but he alerted the marshals to be ready to move.

The Attorney General had driven home to McLean, Virginia, ten miles from the Department of Justice, for lunch. White telephoned him. But like another famous American at another moment of national crisis—General George C. Marshall on Dec. 7, 1941—Robert Kennedy was out riding horseback. White was assured he would return the call the second he walked in.

About this time Guthman, a Pulitzer Prize winning newspaper reporter whose exposé of Teamsters Union graft helped tumble florid, flamboyant old Dave Beck from the presidency of America's largest union, received a second call from Montgomery. The voice on the other end of the line was Seigenthaler's. The mood was not Seigenthaler's.

"How you doing, John?" asked Guthman, having not the slightest inkling of the ordeal Seigenthaler had just come through.

"Not so good," replied the battered Seigenthaler from his Montgomery hospital bed.

John described the riot and his own attack to Guthman. Again Guthman notified White. Although Seigenthaler was intent upon leaving the hospital, White, who knows something of physical violence from his own brilliant years on the gridiron, overruled him.

Kennedy had now returned to his home. He called White, and the Deputy Attorney General spread the situation out before him in detail.

The Attorney General immediately called his brother in the White House. Ten minutes later he got White back on the line and ordered: "Let's get those guys [the marshals] moving!"

The Attorney General dressed in business clothes and hurried back toward town. But on his way in he stopped at a playing field along the Potomac River. FBI agents were about to begin a baseball game. Robert Kennedy had promised to throw in the first ball. He kept that promise—at 3 p.m. of a day when he was about to take one of the most dramatic steps in the history of race relations in the United States.

When he got to his office about 3:15 p.m., there were more telephone conferences between him and the President, and between assistants to both men.

John F. Kennedy then issued the public statement that placed his brother in full command of the Alabama crisis. He declared:

> The situation which has developed in Alabama is a source of the deepest concern to me, as it must be to a vast majority of the citizens of Alabama and other Americans. I have instructed the Justice Department to take all necessary steps based on their investigation and information.
>
> I call upon the State Governor and other responsible officials in Alabama as well as the Mayors of Birmingham and Montgomery to exercise their lawful authority to prevent any further outbreaks of violence. I would also hope that any persons, whether a citizen of Alabama or a visitor there, would refrain from any action which would in any way tend to provoke further outbreaks.
>
> I hope that State and local officials in Alabama will meet their responsibilities. The U. S. government intends to meet its.

The decision to intervene in Alabama could not have been an easy one for John F. Kennedy. His election six months earlier had been determined by the votes of the near-solid South. His legislative program then before Congress depended in large part upon support from the moderates among Dixie's delegation in House and Senate. He also was just ten days away from departure for his first meeting at the Summit with Soviet Premier Nikita Khrushchev, a wily old propagandist who has exploited American racial problems to his great advantage in Asia and Africa. The need for Federal intervention to protect Negroes in the South would only make those racial problems look more sordid abroad.

But once the decision had been made, the Attorney

General was swift to utilize the authority his brother had granted him to "take all necessary steps" to restore law and order in Alabama.

When he arrived at the Department, he found that 303 Federal law-enforcement officers were ready to go into Montgomery—20 marshals in the District of Columbia; 83 Bureau of Prisons guards; 100 Alcohol Tax officers; and 100 deputy marshals from Southern states. There were 200 more Alcohol Tax men ready to move in the following day. Kennedy ordered the 303 men into Montgomery immediately.

He wired his decision to Patterson and recounted for the reluctant Governor all of the fruitless attempts the Government had made for one week to force Alabama to protect the Freedom Riders. He pointed out that even on that Saturday afternoon he was unable to make contact with Patterson by telephone.

Kennedy's moves were these: The Federal law-enforcement officers were dispatched to Montgomery. Deputy Attorney General Byron White was sent along to be in charge of the operation. The FBI was ordered to send in an extra team "to intensify its investigation of the incident in Montgomery and other events this past week," and an injunction was obtained from Federal District Judge Frank M. Johnson, Jr., in Montgomery to prevent the Ku Klux Klan, the National States Rights Party and other individuals and groups from "interfering with peaceful interstate travel by buses."

Kennedy telephoned Seigenthaler in the Montgomery hospital to express his regrets over the beating and to inform him of the action he had taken.

Seigenthaler described the riot to his boss, and added: "It's damned regrettable this thing happened. I shouldn't have been there and shouldn't have gotten out of the car."

"There's not another thing you could have done," replied Kennedy.

As the conversation was about to end, Seigenthaler had a bit of advice for Kennedy that delighted the Attorney General in an hour when a little mirth was needed. "Don't ever run for Governor of Alabama," said John. "It's a hell of a job."

Although Robert Kennedy and the President were outraged at Patterson's inertia, an investigation of the outburst of violence at the bus terminal indicated to the Attorney General that the Governor himself may have been double-crossed by Montgomery police. There was evidence to show that instead of following Patterson's instructions to protect the Freedom Riders upon their arrival in Montgomery, the police deliberately put in an appearance ten to fifteen minutes late. Their purported plan was to give the mob ten minutes alone with the mixed-racial group—enough time to rough up and frighten the students without killing any. Yet death could have come swiftly to any one of the Freedom Riders, to Seigenthaler or to an innocent bystander in the wild state of anarchy that existed in Montgomery that day.

When Byron White met with Patterson in Montgomery that night, the Governor vehemently denounced Federal intervention. "Your action is illegal, unconstitutional, and worsening the situation," bellowed the Governor, "and it's an insult to the great state of Alabama."

Patterson also warned White that he would arrest any U. S. marshal who broke the laws of Alabama.

White, whose conversational tone normally is not much more audible than the paws of a kitten prancing over a deep-tufted carpet, explained in his subdued, unemotional manner that the Federal marshals were there for only one reason—to protect the rights and lives of individuals who sought to travel from state to state on a public vehicle.

Robert Kennedy meanwhile was using the telephone as a chain smoker uses cigarettes—talking with the President, with White, with Negro leaders, with Southerners, with others in the Government. He remained in his office until Sunday, May 21, when Montgomery appeared to have settled into a temporary early morning calm.

After a few hours of sleep, the Attorney General attended Mass, and returned to his office. Montgomery once more was about to explode, but with an even more powerful wallop than before, because the Reverend Martin Luther King, thirty-two-year-old national head of the Southern Christian Leadership Conference, was on his way into that beleaguered city.

The Attorney General had been in communication with King since things first grew tense in Alabama. He had made a futile attempt to persuade King to stay away from Montgomery.

King, the high priest of the passive resistance movement that Negroes have adopted as their most effective weapon against discrimination and segregation, had to assume the leadership role in Alabama or face the possibility of losing his command. He also believed that Negroes had gained an impressive psychological victory in Montgomery and could not afford to retreat or falter.

As Sunday evening approached in Montgomery, with King on hand to lead the young militants, tension mounted toward the point of explosion.

The Freedom Riders gathered with King in the First Baptist Church. An angry mob began to assemble outside the church. Kennedy's law-enforcement team was there to keep order. The team at that point included only about 150 men. But twice that many were on their way to Montgomery.

The Attorney General himself maintained his vigil in Washington, still utilizing his telephone as an instrument of communication and control. His contact with the President and with White was frequent. On Sunday he also established communications with King, inside the church. He still could not reach Patterson.

There was no mistaking the intent of the rampaging mob. It was massacre if the race-haters could get hold of King and his brethren. It was cremation if they could not, for they appeared intent upon burning the Negro church and the Freedom Riders with it. Patterson, sitting in Montgomery, was as fully aware of the crowd's evil determination as was Kennedy in Washington.

Finally, at 1:35 a.m. on Monday, May 22, the weary, somewhat haggard Attorney General received the last of a series of telephone calls that the governor made to him through the harrowing night, beginning at 8:30 p.m. Sunday. Patterson was shouting so loudly into the telephone that the assistants gathered with Kennedy in his office could hear every word he said. Ed Guthman, who was across the desk from Kennedy, scratched off a note while the Governor bloviated. It read: "Patterson still thinks that the Justice Department is sending the Freedom Riders in there."

Patterson had informed Kennedy in his first angry telephone call, at 8:30 p.m. Sunday, that he had ordered out the Alabama National Guard to quell the riot. But apparently he felt additional need to vent his wrath at Kennedy over the telephone. When he called at 1:35 a.m., Patterson bellowed over and over to Kennedy: "You sent them down here."

Kennedy, maintaining a slightly sardonic and humorous manner with the Governor, replied: "You know that isn't true, John. I don't care if that's what you tell your people down there on television, John, but don't tell me that."

For twenty-five minutes the lines between Montgomery and Washington echoed with Patterson's thunder and Bobby Kennedy's subdued but brittle sarcasm.

The Governor demanded withdrawal of Federal officers on grounds that their presence was causing "a very serious political situation and doing great harm to the Democratic party."

Kennedy kayoed this argument with a single verbal punch. "It is more important that the people survive physically than that we survive politically," he told Patterson.

Patterson then contended that his National Guard could protect all of King's congregation, but not King himself. He said this was the judgment of Adjutant General Henry Graham who had taken command of the military force at the church.

"You have the General call me," replied Kennedy irately, "I want him to say that to me. I want to hear a General of the United States Army say he can't protect Martin Luther King."

Patterson reversed his path. He agreed that Graham could safeguard King. With that declaration the conversation ended.

Minutes later Kennedy received a call from King.

As he picked up the telephone, Kennedy asked with an impish lilt in his voice: "Well, Reverend, are you praying for us?"

King was not in a lighthearted mood. Graham had announced to the congregation that his forces had taken over protection of the church and that the Freedom Riders were to remain there until morning.

The dark-skinned evangelist of integration's cause had serious doubts whether Patterson's National

Guard would protect him and the Freedom Riders. Kennedy assured him it would.

He also expressed some doubts about the ability of Kennedy's marshals to keep the mob in check.

"Now, Reverend," said Kennedy with the same cool and dispassionate inflection he had used on Patterson, "you know that without those Federal marshals all of you would be as dead as doornails."

When the night of crisis ended and the Freedom Riders were hustled to safety away from the church, on Monday morning, Kennedy dispatched 200 more Federal officers into Alabama. White reported to him that day: "There's a hell of a potential for violence yet. As a practical matter we have the city of Montgomery in hand—but it's a big state."

Robert Kennedy began that day thinking about calling for a cooling-off period, but he could not find the proper words for his appeal without appearing to pull the rug from under the Freedom Riders.

He also had started consultations with Mississippi's Governor Ross Barnett and Senator Jim Eastland to be sure that there would not be a recurrence in their state of the violence that swept Alabama.

Tuesday, May 23, was a day of negotiation with both sides and of watchful waiting. Kennedy's marshals still were on duty, ready to bring any new attempt at mob rule to a swift halt.

Wednesday, May 24, was a day of action. The Freedom Riders began their journey from Montgomery to Jackson, Mississippi, their bus so heavily guarded that it would have required a full-scale military operation for opponents to harm them. Behind them rode a second bus, unprotected and filled with people who had had no role in the tragic events of the previous days.

The second bus nearly fell under attack by fanatics who thought it contained a mixed racial group. Although the attack was not carried out, the very possibility that it could have happened forced Robert Kennedy's hand. He decided the opportunity for violence was too great—especially violence that could be done innocent individuals who were not partisans in the bitter dispute over the Freedom Riders.

At 4 p.m. Wednesday, the Attorney General issued a public statement, pointing up the inherent dangers that lurked in a situation where "curiosity seekers, publicity seekers and others seeking to serve their own causes" had burst in upon the South along with the Freedom Riders.

He declared: "In this confused situation, there is increasing possibility that innocent persons may be injured. A mob asks no questions.

"The Alabama and Mississippi law-enforcement officials are meeting the test today, but their job is becoming increasingly difficult."

Kennedy said "a cooling-off period is needed." He added: "It would be wise for those traveling through these two states to delay their trips until the present state of confusion and danger has passed and an atmosphere of reason and normalcy has been restored."

The move angered Negro leaders and they flatly rejected it. King, in a telephone conversation with Guthman the previous evening, had vowed there would be no retreat. "This is a turning point and a testing point," King told Guthman. "Little Rock was the psychological turning point as far as school desegregation was concerned. If we can break the back of opposition here [Alabama], public facilities will be desegregated tomorrow."

Kennedy's bid for a cooling-off period came as the State of Mississippi slapped twelve Freedom Riders— those who had made the heavily guarded trip from

Montgomery—into jail in Jackson. This, in Kennedy's mind, was the way the matter should be handled. It should be settled by the courts and not forcibly by a howling mob, National Guard troops or Federal marshals.

Barnett had done a superb job of protecting the Riders until he could put them under arrest. Once they had been arrested and the basis for court action had been established, Mississippi authorities notified the Attorney General that they could be freed if they would end their activities.

Kennedy reported this information to King, who still was in Montgomery. The conversation began at 9:15 p.m. Wednesday, May 24.

The Attorney General was greatly concerned over the effect further demonstrations and need for Federal interference would have on the President's meeting at the Summit with Khrushchev and on world opinion at a moment of grave international tension over Berlin.

An immediate release from jail and swift cessation of Freedom Rider activities in the South was not part of King's plan. He told Kennedy that as long as the group remained in jail, other integrationists would move into the South. He maintained also that it was part of the philosophy of the passive resistance movement that its young disciples should remain in jail—much as Ghandi had in India.

Kennedy was firm and fervent in his attempt to enlist King's support for his position. He told the minister that if he was interested in the welfare of the nation at a time when it stood in peril he had an obligation to prevent further racial distress in the South.

King responded that he and those who followed him in the passionate quest for equality had to continue their struggle. "It's a matter of conscience and morality," said King. "They will use their lives and their bodies to right a wrong. They will give witness by their lives if necessary."

It was a moral obligation of those who had enlisted in the nonviolent drive to wipe out racial segregation to accept whatever penalty is given them, said King.

Although Kennedy has high regard for King as an intelligent and responsible leader of his people, he became impatient with King's adamancy. It was an impatience born of Robert Kennedy's simple basic philosophy that law and order must prevail, that the national interest is paramount to all others, that the beating of drums and the flailing of arms is so much lost motion when issues can be settled in an orderly and quiet way without attention-attracting antics.

He admired the courage of the first Freedom Riders and believed they had performed a service to the Negro race and their nation by focusing a raw, hot spotlight upon the segregation practiced in interstate travel facilities. He was convinced that now the time had arrived for the spotlight to be turned off.

He bluntly informed King that further suffering and attempts at martyrdom by his followers "will not have the slightest effect on what the Government is going to do in this field or any other."

King threatened to summon 100,000 students into Alabama. The move was miscalculated. People may scoff at Robert Kennedy's youth and inexperience. They may criticize his lack of emotional identification with the more pressing social problems of the era. They may label him his brother's "hatchet man." But, as Ed Guthman succinctly states it, "You don't threaten Bob Kennedy!"

"This country belongs to you as much as to me," said the Attorney General—stating the situation as he saw it, in the most simple and naked terms of good and evil.

He pointed out that King could determine as much as he could where America was going. Then, a bit sadly, Kennedy added: "This is not the way to deal with us."

King's manner changed. He now realized that he had to attempt to impress Kennedy with the deep, religious fervor that drove his followers along their route. "It is difficult for others to understand the position of an oppressed people . . . ours is a way out. . . . It is creative, moral and nonviolent."

To Kennedy's contention that the national interest could not be served by further demonstration, King replied that Negroes would not turn to black supremacy or to communism if his movement proved successful. He maintained that if the problem of racial discrimination was solved in the near future it would "save the soul of America."

But, said King, he "deeply appreciated" the manner in which the Kennedy Administration was handling civil rights and saw "a ray of hope" in its actions.

The telephone conversation ended. The Freedom Riders eventually left their Jackson jail cells. Their case was taken into court. On May 29, Robert Kennedy petitioned the Interstate Commerce Commission to issue regulations prohibiting segregation in interstate bus transportation.

Guthman says: "Alabama was the best test of Bob Kennedy. He never once got emotionally involved. Whatever his personal feelings were, he looked at the situation rather coldly. His judgment never faltered."

Byron White stated later that the Federal Government's firm stand in Montgomery put local communities on notice that they had to maintain law and order in disputes arising from the desegregation of travel facilities. In the next fourteen months, the Justice Department found itself embroiled in a number of disputes over "Freedom Riders" in the South. But the bloody violence of Montgomery was not repeated. White said the Eisenhower Administration's action in Little Rock in 1957 accomplished the same goal for school integration that Montgomery did for the desegregation of travel facilities.

The Kennedys were blistered by much of the Southern press for their intervention on behalf of the embattled Freedom Riders. The *Shreveport Journal* accused them of "playing into the Communists' hands by encouraging race-mixers to try to impose themselves upon the white people of the South." The *Montgomery Journal* said the sending of marshals into Alabama was "another example of the youthful adolescence of the Attorney General and the impropriety of having a man of his age and prejudices in the highest law-enforcement office in the land."

But, for all its vehemence over the entry of Federal marshals into its city, *The Montgomery Advertiser* most clearly and honestly stated the tragedy of the situation in an editorial on May 23, 1961. After attacking Patterson's vacillation and Kennedy's action, that newspaper declared: "But when all that has been said, we Montgomerians and Alabamians are left in loneliness and with a grievous problem. The agitators will be tried for defiance of Alabama law.

"But what of the mobsters who have defied Alabama law? They were not duly quelled and that failure is ours alone. In fact, the mobsters were encouraged."

The racial battle of Alabama occurred just a few weeks after the disastrous attempt by Cuban rebels to invade their communist-dominated country and at a time when a citizens committee headed by Mrs. Eleanor Roosevelt, United Auto Workers President Walter Reuther and Dr. Milton Eisenhower was attempting to raise money to purchase tractors which were to be traded to Fidel Castro for the rebel prisoners he held.

Many Southern publications lumped Montgomery and Cuba together in attacking the Kennedys.

The Grand Dragon of the Ku Klux Klan of Arkansas had a rather special approach. He wrote a one-sentence letter to the Attorney General: "Please advise if you would be interested in the following proposal: I offer to trade one Freedom Rider for one tractor."

Robert Kennedy shies away from a direct comparison between his moves in Montgomery and those of President Eisenhower in the violent Little Rock uprising. He merely states his belief that it was wiser to utilize U. S. marshals to enforce the law than to send in helmeted, armed troops as Eisenhower did.

"Something had to be done," says the Attorney General, looking at Montgomery in retrospect, "and I don't think it was necessary to send in troops."

Late in January, 1962, as he was preparing to leave on an around-the-world goodwill tour, the Attorney General sat in his office talking about his first year in the Cabinet. He was asked what he regarded as his major achievements in that period.

"I think that in two areas that are particularly controversial we made some progress—civil rights and organized crime," said Kennedy.

He added: "We made greater progress than I had anticipated we would in the area of organized crime. We took a step forward. I originally felt it would take that long—a whole year—just to get things going."

"In civil rights, I think we had great accomplishment, and bitterness and hatred were not engendered throughout the country. This is important."

The Attorney General said he had not found it difficult serving in the dual role of Cabinet member and brother to the President; nor had he come across many surprises between January 20, 1961, and January 20, 1962. "It was just a year's experience," he said.

A few weeks earlier, in an official report to the President, the Attorney General summarized his Department's activities in civil rights, pointing with particular pride to strides taken toward abolishing racial discrimination in voting, employment, transportation and public education.

He stated that the Department had filed fourteen new cases charging discrimination in the voter registration processes and had, at the end of 1961, investigations or negotiations with local officials being conducted in sixty-one other counties. "Our effort is to discover and eliminate all racial discrimination in the voting processes," said Robert Kennedy.

He cited the fact that the number of Negro attorneys in his Department had increased from ten to fifty during the year and that many Negroes had been appointed to high posts, including the first two ever named as United States Attorneys—Cecil F. Poole in California and Merle M. McCurdy in Ohio.

The Attorney General pointed out that in the fall of 1961 schools in many Southern communities, including Atlanta, New Orleans, Little Rock, Memphis and Dallas, were integrated and "for the first time since the Supreme Court's desegregation decision in 1954 there was no violence or disrespect for the law."

"In school integration there has been a basic change in policy from abstention by the Federal Government, except during crisis or a disaster, to affirmative anticipatory action," said Kennedy in direct criticism of his predecessor's action—or inaction.

"We have done this to preserve court orders and to prevent violence," he added. "This Administration has moved with vigor in all cases to protect the integrity of the court, to preserve due administration of justice and to encourage and assist local officials and community leaders who are charged with the responsibility in the desegregation of schools."

Turning to the question of segregated transportation, Robert Kennedy stated that since May, 1961—when the first Freedom Riders blazed their tortured trail through the South—the Department had made "substantial progress toward eliminating discrimination in all three major modes of public transportation—bus, air and rail."

He cited his order to send 600 U. S. marshals into Montgomery and said it was necessitated by the fact that "local officials in Alabama either could not or would not maintain order."

"The Government had a clear responsibility to protect interstate travelers," said the Attorney General. "The presence of the marshals averted major bloodshed and it was unnecessary to take further action a few days later when a similarly tense situation developed in Mississippi. Immediately after it became apparent that local officials had the situation under control, the marshals were withdrawn."

Robert Kennedy pointed out also that the Interstate Commerce Commission, after being petitioned by the Justice Department, issued regulations, effective November 1, 1961, requiring desegregated facilities in terminals used in interstate bus travel. Although segregation signs were removed from terminals in McComb and Greenwood, Mississippi, as a result of this order, the Department had to file six other actions to require compliance with Federal law.

As a result of negotiations with the Department, eighteen railroads had agreed to desegregate several hundred terminals in the South, said Kennedy. He also explained that the Department had filed suits in New Orleans and Montgomery to eliminate air-terminal segregation.

In the spring of 1962, the Attorney General led the fight for Congressional approval of legislation to abolish literacy tests as qualifications for voting.

Such a record would appear impressive on the surface. But many leaders of the Negro community felt the Attorney General had not gone as far as he should to wipe out racial discrimination.

Clarence Mitchell, director of the Washington Bureau for the National Association for the Advancement of Colored People, speaking in an interview, commended Robert Kennedy for his enforcement of the Federal statute against discrimination at the polls and his proposal to abolish literacy tests as a requirement for voting.

But Mitchell was critical of the Attorney General for not proposing and fighting for new civil rights legislation to speed desegregation in the South and for his reliance on local officials in Southern states to enforce the law.

The Negro leader, who has been at the center of the fight for civil rights for many years, said: "In my opinion, the Attorney General has been constructively active in a high number of areas. But the big difficulty is that he has not come forward with any proposals for new legislation."

It was Mitchell's opinion also that Robert Kennedy handled the Freedom Riders incident in Alabama badly because he relied in the beginning on state officials to prevent violence.

The Eisenhower Administration scored a more impressive victory in Little Rock when it called out the National Guard to enforce school integration, said Mitchell.

"It is my opinion that this really was one of the most healthy things that could have happened to forestall state-sanctioned violence," said Mitchell. "The Southern states thought they could use the National Guard to protect violence. But after Little Rock they knew they could not use the National Guard for this purpose. President Eisenhower saved the nation from serious anarchy."

He added: "Historically marshals are not as impressive as troops."

Mitchell repeatedly emphasized that although the Kennedy Administration had made moves to end segregation in public transportation, individuals who flaunted Southern laws against integration still were being arrested. He maintained that the Attorney General should urge passage of a Fair Employment Practices Act and legislation which would give him authority to seek injunctions to halt all segregation in public facilities.

"There isn't any question but that the two Kennedys —the President and the Attorney General—have a fresh and new appearance on some of these things," said the NAACP leader. "But I don't believe they put civil rights as high on their agenda as many people think they do. They have other political considerations, like Federal aid to education and medical care for the aged."

Mitchell credits Robert Kennedy with having moved more constructively and decisively than his predecessor, William Rogers, in attempting to enforce the voting laws.

Mitchell and other proponents of strong civil rights action feel, however, that the President and the Attorney General have sacrificed such action in an effort to win Southern congressional support for other legislative measures and to weld together a Democratic party that will be impregnable at the polls—in both North and South.

Months after peace had settled once more over Alabama, Robert Kennedy had had no contact with his one-time friend and political ally, Governor Patterson. He had, however, maintained a cordial relationship with Martin Luther King and had been visited by the personable minister in his office several times.

Throughout the ordeal of Montgomery, Robert Kennedy performed his duties with a deliberate objectivity that placed enforcement of Federal law and protection of human life above all other considerations. Those who watched the performance at its various stages through eleven hectic days—and they include his own aides, newspaper reporters, and antagonists on both sides of the dispute—were impressed by Kennedy's ability to make vital decisions calmly and without vacillation or self-doubt.

Although he never was out of contact with the President for very long, Robert Kennedy spoke and acted with the authority of the Presidency itself.

When John Kennedy was asked at his July 19, 1961, press conference to state his personal opinion of the Freedom Riders and their sorties into the South, he left no doubt that Robert Kennedy's words and deeds reflected completely his own views.

"I think the Attorney General has made it clear that we believe that everyone who travels for whatever reason they travel should enjoy the full Constitutional protection given to them by the law and by the Constitution," said the President. "They should be able to move freely in interstate commerce."

No previous Attorney General and few former cabinet officers—one possible exception being the late Secretary of State John Foster Dulles—ever possessed and exercised the sweeping power that was Robert Kennedy's in that time of domestic crisis.

This unusual circumstance of one brother utilizing the authority of another had the advantage of keeping John F. Kennedy himself off the firing line. When the smoke had settled over Montgomery, there were many on both sides of the bitter controversy who looked with disfavor upon the President's brother. Few, however, felt recrimination against the President himself.

Pollster Samuel Lubell, touring the Deep South one month after the Montgomery blow-up, reported: "On the whole . . . the Freedom Riders do not seem to have hurt President Kennedy much in the South. The American voter has always made excuses for presidents he likes, and it is 'Brother Bobby' in the Attorney General's office, rather than President Jack, who has been blamed for how the Alabama bus violence was handled."

To punctuate his conclusion, Lubell quoted a Birmingham fireman as stating: "I don't blame Jack, but that Bobby is out for trouble."

Chapter Nine
Adventures Together

SITTING AT THE DESK IMMEDIATELY OUTSIDE THE DOOR TO President Kennedy's private office in the west wing of the White House is the only man who has been an active participant in each of the political and professional adventures undertaken together by the Brothers Kennedy.

He is Kenneth O'Donnell, a slim, athletic New Frontiersman possessed of steel-hard mental and physical faculties not unlike those of the Kennedys themselves. He is a former captain of the Harvard football team and the father of five. He also is a member of that elite corps of Kennedy insiders.

Ken O'Donnell also is one of Robert Kennedy's closest friends.

As special assistant to the President, O'Donnell screens and arranges all of John Kennedy's official appointments, talks with many people the Chief Executive is unable to see, relieves the President of myriad major and minor tasks that otherwise would consume his valuable time, and acts as his traveling companion and personal assistant on trips away from Washington.

When Robert Kennedy was chief counsel for the Senate Rackets Committee, O'Donnell occupied a desk beside the door to his office and performed a similar assortment of administrative, investigative and research jobs that lifted a heavy burden off Robert Kennedy.

Kenneth O'Donnell probably has a better understanding than anyone outside the Kennedy family of the interdependence of John and Robert Kennedy. "The guy you trust most is your own brother," says O'Donnell, discussing the younger Kennedy's role in the Administration. "Others must have their own independent views. But from Bobby the President gets opinion that is uncolored. In the CIA investigation after Cuba he could be sure with Bobby on the committee that he had someone there who represented him personally."

Before joining the Kennedys on the Rackets Committee, O'Donnell had worked with them on Jack's 1952 senatorial campaign and his unsuccessful vice-presidential bid in 1956. From the Rackets Committee, O'Donnell went directly into Jack's 1958 senatorial fight, then into the presidential campaign and finally to the White House.

Although he had known Robert Kennedy since their

Harvard days, Ken had not worked with him until 1952. "In January, 1952, Bob called me and said Jack was thinking of running statewide and would I help," O'Donnell recalls. "I agreed to help."

Ken's memories of Robert's role in the 1952 political fight are much the same as those of the President. He says that long before Jack officially got into the race he had decided to manage his own campaign. But as difficulties were compounded, he finally brought his brother in as manager, and the whole atmosphere changed. "Bob is a really good organizer," says O'Donnell.

Robert Kennedy, Ken O'Donnell, and Lawrence F. O'Brien, the wise and likable political magician who now is the President's liaison chief with Congress, put together a kind of campaign operation Massachusetts never had seen. Although they were branded political amateurs, they got thousands of persons who never before had been in politics to do volunteer work and recruited local secretaries—about 350 of them—to be in charge of every community of 600 or more in the state. They added 100,000 new names to the voter registration lists.

In addition to acting as manager for this amazing organization, Robert Kennedy helped his mother, his wife, and his sisters campaign for Jack. One night he dashed from headquarters to a nearby rally to deliver this succinct oration:

"My brother Jack couldn't be here. My mother couldn't be here. My sister Eunice couldn't be here, my sister Pat couldn't be here, my sister Jean couldn't be here, but if my brother Jack were here he'd tell you Lodge has a very bad voting record. Thank you."

Robert Kennedy has had to perform unpleasant tasks in the campaigns he has run for his brother but probably few were more unpleasant than being forced to inform Massachusetts' able and popular governor, Paul Dever, that Jack Kennedy would not join campaign forces with him in 1952. Dever, seeking re-election, was tied up with old-line political elements in the state and also had made a rather poor showing when he keynoted the Democratic national convention that year. Dever normally made an outstanding platform appearance. But he was a short, heavy-set man not built for television, and in addition he suffered a bad case of laryngitis at the Chicago convention. Standing beneath hot lights and speaking in a hoarse voice, Dever looked and sounded like a typical Boston machine politician.

Many Massachusetts political observers believe that that speech alone defeated Dever for re-election against Christian A. Herter. He may also have been hurt by Kennedy independence. The Kennedys decided to run their own show—their way and alone. It fell to Robert Kennedy, in a meeting at the Ritz Carlton Hotel, to tell this to the Governor. Dever did not like it. But there was nothing he could do. Here, again, the younger Kennedy played the role of tough guy.

Election night, 1952, was long and tense. Jack Kennedy won the usually lopsided vote that Boston gives to Democrats. But as the night wore on, the outstate tally cut deeply into this margin. Robert Kennedy, working a slide rule and consulting past statistics, saw a glimmer of hope, however, even as Jack's Boston lead dwindled. Lodge was running big outstate, but apparently not big enough. The tremendous organizational work that Robert Kennedy, Ken O'Donnell and Larry O'Brien had done in the cities and towns removed from Greater Boston was paying off. Although Dwight D. Eisenhower carried the state by 208,000 votes over Adlai E. Stevenson and Herter beat Dever by 25,000, it became apparent as the sun rose on the morning after election day that Jack Kennedy had defeated Lodge. His margin was 70,000 votes.

At the beginning of 1953, Jack began his service as junior Senator from Massachusetts and Robert Kennedy joined the McCarthy Subcommittee. Not until 1956 did the brothers again join in another political venture. In the spring of that year, New England—and especially Massachusetts—began stirring with talk of Jack Kennedy for Vice President. The Kennedys themselves were interested—all except Joseph P. Kennedy who opposed the idea. But there was not a great deal that could be done prior to the Chicago convention of mid-August. It is traditional that the presidential nominee choose his own running mate. Still there were inklings weeks before the convention that Adlai Stevenson—who by early summer was assured the presidential nomination—might let the convention itself decide the issue. No one knew for sure what would happen.

Jack Kennedy's people, including his brother, began talking about his vice-presidential candidacy among state leaders and delegates, explaining that if Stevenson let the convention make the decision, Jack would appreciate their support.

When the Kennedys got to convention, there still was no decision. But Jack got two good breaks. First he appeared before the convention to narrate a Democratic propaganda film put together by Dore Schary, who later wrote *Sunrise at Campobello*. He also was chosen to place Stevenson's name in nomination.

Finally, after Stevenson won the nomination, he announced he had decided "that the selection of the vice-presidential nominee should be made through the free process of this convention."

The Kennedys jumped into the fight. Also seeking the nomination were Senator Hubert Humphrey of

Minnesota; Senators Estes Kefauver and Albert Gore of Tennessee; Mayor Robert Wagner of New York and others.

Robert Kennedy, his sisters and Jack's old college mates and Senate aides worked all night long, buttonholing delegates. Their drive was so makeshift and impromptu that they even had difficulty finding the proper politicians to second the nominating speech to be made on Jack's behalf by Governor Abraham Ribicoff of Connecticut. Robert went to House Majority leader John McCormack, Jack's old intraparty foe from Boston, and asked him to second the nomination. McCormack was a bitter anti-Kennedyite for many reasons. Kennedy had incurred McCormack's wrath when, as a young Congressman, he refused to sign a petition asking President Truman to pardon Boston's flamboyant old political boss, James Michael Curley, and again early in 1956 when he wrested control of the state Democratic party from McCormack.

Robert Kennedy talked with McCormack on the convention floor, but was unable to persuade him to make the speech. One observer recalls that after McCormack made clear his refusal, Kennedy sarcastically replied, "Thanks, Congressman," and strode away in anger. Moments later, McCormack reconsidered and ended up going through the motions of seconding the nomination, although his entire speech dealt not with Jack Kennedy's qualifications but with the solid political need to nominate a New Englander.

Robert, Ken O'Donnell and other Kennedyites were all over the floor as the balloting proceeded. Jack remained in his suite at the Stockyards Inn.

Although the Kennedy operation was impromptu and not well organized, it worked surprisingly well. The third ballot became a showdown between Kennedy and Kefauver. Robert Kennedy doggedly and persuasively moved from delegation to delegation. Jack got within 38½ votes of victory. Then McCormack dashed to the rostrum, shouting to his old House colleague and convention chairman, the late Speaker Sam Rayburn of Texas, to recognize Missouri. The question always will remain whether he knew Missouri was going to swing to Kefauver or whether he thought it was going to Kennedy. Plenty of on-the-spot spectators will swear to the veracity of either version. Whatever McCormack's motive, Rayburn recognized Missouri, the floodgates opened for Kefauver and Kennedy was through.

Robert Kennedy recalls that moment on the convention floor as one of the most disappointing of his life. But by the time he got to Jack's hotel room, he had bolstered his own spirits and was able to tell his brother: "This is the luckiest thing that ever happened to you."

He was right, of course. Had Jack Kennedy won the vice-presidential nomination, he could not have stopped Ike's slaughter of Stevenson in the November election. But he would have been blamed in large part for it because he is a Catholic. His own presidential ambitions might have been damaged irreparably.

After the convention, Robert Kennedy joined the Stevenson campaign as an aide to the campaign director, the late James Finnegan. He traveled across the nation with Adlai Stevenson for seven weeks and learned some sound political lessons that later paid off heavily in his stewardship of Jack's presidential campaign.

"Starting at the convention," he says, "I learned two major lessons. First, in our own struggle for the vice-presidency, we didn't have communications between the delegates and the people who were interested in us. I said at the time that if we ever got involved again, we would have communications. Secondly, I learned that friendship is of utmost importance. It made a far greater difference than anything else. Estes Kefauver had visited people and sent out cards and this is what paid off."

From 1956 on Jack Kennedy also visited people and in addition sent out thousands of Christmas cards, letters and copies of his book, *Profiles in Courage,* to prospective 1960 convention delegates and political powers.

Robert Kennedy also watched the Stevenson campaign devolve into a shambles. The candidate spent far too many hours poring over weighty speeches. He showed his distaste for hand-shaking, whistle-stopping and off-the-cuff speeches. He often discussed some far-off foreign problem with voters who had come to hear what he planned to do about their own bread-and-butter worries. He occasionally kept audiences waiting unnecessarily. His press relations reached the disaster point. He ruined eloquent television speeches by rushing through final pages at jet speed rather than abandoning them when air time was about to run out. He also utilized costly network time to address a million or two persons when he should have been reaching as many as fifteen million. His command was bitterly divided between Finnegan, the campaign manager, and the late Paul Butler, the Democratic national chairman.

Robert Kennedy, who already was thinking of the presidential bid his brother would make four years later, determined that he and Jack would not make similar mistakes.

After Stevenson's resounding defeat, Robert returned to his duties as chief counsel for the Permanent Investigations Subcommittee and within days was off on the adventure that would make him a national figure.

Clark Mollenhoff, a brusque, hard-hitting reporter

for the *Des Moines Register and Tribune* who later won a Pulitzer Prize for his relentless pursuit of labor racketeers, had suggested to him the previous summer that he investigate corruption within the nation's biggest and most powerful union, the Teamsters International. Robert Kennedy was reluctant because two previous congressional investigations had been made of the Teamsters without digging up much dirt and because he did not think his subcommittee had jurisdiction over the matter. But Mollenhoff, a persuasive and reliable reporter, convinced him that the other two investigations "were fixed" and that the McClellan Subcommittee had jurisdiction because the Teamsters were misusing tax-exempt funds.

Kennedy talked the matter over with McClellan and got the chairman's approval to begin a preliminary investigation. With the aid of Carmine Bellino, the subcommittee's chief accountant, and trips to Los Angeles, Seattle and Chicago, Kennedy amassed some shocking evidence against the union during the months of November and December, 1956. He discovered to his own surprise that corruption in the Teamsters was not limited to lesser figures, but began at the very top, with Dave Beck, the president. He found that Beck, a florid, ill-tempered old unionist who enjoyed nationwide respectability and had visited President Eisenhower in the White House, had tapped the till in some rather ingenious ways to provide funds for the high living he loved.

Robert Kennedy laid his evidence before McClellan. The Arkansas Democrat recognized its importance and the need for a probe, but questioned whether the subcommittee had jurisdiction. About the same time, the late Senator Irving Ives of New York began urging the Senate Labor Committee to investigate union misdoings. There also were fears in the Senate and among labor leaders that if the balance of power at mid-term shifted from Democrats, who had a one-vote margin in the Senate, to the Republicans, the late Senator Joseph McCarthy of Wisconsin would become chairman of McClellan's subcommittee. All of these problems were resolved when the Senate set up the Select Committee on Improper Activities in the Labor or Management Field, with four Democratic and four Republican members, McClellan as chairman and Ives as vice chairman. One of the Democratic members was John Kennedy.

The chief counsel was Robert Kennedy.

Once the committee was established, a $350,000 appropriation voted, and a full staff assigned to probe the misdoings of men and women on both sides of the labor-management picture, the scene was set for one of the most startling, most fairly operated and best organized investigations in the history of Congress. When it later turned out certain Teamsters were squandering union funds, Robert Kennedy was off and running.

His investigators fanned out across the country, digging and scratching for every bit of information they could find that would trace corruption, terrorism, underworld alliances, violence, collusion with management, and petty theft to entrenched leaders of organized labor, both big and small.

The men and women who paraded before the committee in the great, ornate Senate caucus room—and at the same time across television screens in millions of American homes—formed the most colorful cast of characters ever assembled for a congressional probe. It was a cast Damon Runyon would have coveted. Beck, Nathan Shefferman, "Big Helen," and "Little Helen," two "business" ladies from the Pacific Northwest. Rough, handsome Johnny Dio, from New York. Frank Brewster, the dapper, debonair Teamsters boss in

Seattle. A vocal Vesuvius named Tony Doria, who bellowed for hours before the committee. George Bender, a former United States Senator. James G. Cross, who headed the Bakery and Confectionery Workers Union. Sam Goldstein, Martin Lacey, a magnificent old labor warhorse. And Lyman C. Conger, the Kohler Company's angry foe of unionism. There were many others.

Beck was the first and the biggest of labor's monarchs to fall. Robert Kennedy and his investigators hammered the Teamsters President with a battery of records and files that indicated he had used $370,000 from the union treasury to provide himself with a plush life. The proud, tough veteran of decades of bloody labor battles could not fight back. He was forced to retreat behind the fifth amendment, which he invoked in a hoarse voice and belligerent manner and in reply to the simplest questions. His days as chief of the nation's biggest union were at an end.

As the months rolled on, Robert Kennedy and his committee made big trouble for other union leaders who had made big trouble for their respective organizations by robbing the coffers, aligning themselves with hoodlums and gangsters, abolishing constitutional rights, taking payoffs from management, stealing elections and a variety of other evils.

As a result of the rackets probe, Cross and his Bakery and Confectionery Workers Union were ousted from the AFL-CIO; Maurice Hutcheson, president of the Carpenters Union, was indicted for contempt of Congress; William E. Maloney resigned the presidency of the Operating Engineers Union; Lloyd Klenert, secretary-treasurer, and Anthony Valente, president, bowed out of the United Textile Workers of America; Max and Louis Block were forced out of the Meat Cutters Union; and an assortment of Teamsters officials were indicted.

After he became Attorney General, Kennedy continued to haunt some of the characters he had come across in his Rackets Committee days. Metro Holovachka, the Lake County, Indiana, prosecutor who claimed he lacked jurisdiction to indict Hutcheson and others allegedly involved in a state highway swindle, was convicted on charges of income-tax evasion in February, 1962, in northern Indiana Federal District Court. Kennedy's Justice Department prepared the case. "Tony Ducks" Corallo was indicted in December, 1961, along with a New York Supreme Court justice and a former U. S. attorney on charges of trying to influence a Federal judge in a criminal case. Robert Kennedy personally supervised the investigation that led to the indictment.

The American people were shocked for the vivid moment that the rackets probe filled their TV screens at discovering that certain supposedly dedicated labor leaders actually were thieves and the operating partners of gangsters and labor-hating employers. Now that the moment has passed, it probably is safe to state that only one truly indelible impression lingers in the national consciousness of the three-year investigation; that of the monumental hate and endless pursuit by Robert F. Kennedy of a bellicose little labor boss named James Riddle Hoffa.

When the two men first faced each other beneath the magnificent crystal chandeliers in the Senate caucus room, Kennedy was merely counsel for a congressional committee and Hoffa was but a vice president of the Teamsters Union. Today, with Kennedy as Attorney General and number-two man in the United States Government and Hoffa as president of America's most powerful union, the hate is stronger than ever and the pursuit is equally determined. Hoffa escaped Kennedy's net in the John Cye Cheasty bribery case of 1957. He likewise was acquitted in a wire-tap case in 1958. At the end of 1961, he still faced court charges that in a Florida real-estate deal he misused $500,000 in union funds and used the mails to defraud. In the spring of 1962, a Federal Grand Jury indicted Hoffa in Nashville, Tennessee, for allegedly violating the Taft-Hartley Law in a million dollar business deal with a trucking firm. The case stretched back to information acquired by the Rackets Committee in 1957. He knew also that in the administration of John Kennedy, the Justice Department, the Labor Department, the Internal Revenue Service were constantly alert to any misstep he might take.

Hoffa long has boasted of his scheme of empire that would place within his hands the power to withhold food, clothing, police and fire protection and other basic necessities from the American people unless they acquiesce to his demands. He would accomplish this as tsar of all transportation unions and by organizing police, firemen and government workers.

Hoffa first was elected president of the Teamsters in October, 1957, while the McClellan Committee publicly was documenting his sordid record. But a Federal court decreed that he could hold the office only provisionally and designated a board of monitors to oversee his activities. By July, 1961, the monitors were gone and the Teamsters triumphantly, and without provision, elected the forty-eight-year-old Hoffa as their president. Robert Kennedy devoted half of his book, *The Enemy Within,* to tracing the Committee's investigation of Hoffa and his misdeeds. In it, he says:

In 1957 Hoffa promised to clean up the Teamsters if he became president. In 1958 he said he had not had time to do a complete job. In 1959 he said the Teamsters were clean. Hoffa has abandoned any pretense that he will clean up. He has not—and because of the men around him, he cannot.

The Teamsters Union is the most powerful institution in this country—aside from the United States Government itself. In many major metropolitan areas the Teamsters control all transportation. It is a Teamster who drives the mother to the hospital at birth. It is a Teamster who drives the hearse at death. And between birth and burial, the Teamsters drive the trucks that clothe and feed us and provide the vital necessities of life. They control the pickup and deliveries of milk, frozen meat, fresh fruit, department store merchandise, newspapers, railroad express, air freight, and of cargo to and from the sea docks.

Quite literally your life—and the life of every person in the United States—is in the hands of Hoffa and his Teamsters.

But, though the great majority of Teamster officers and Teamster members are honest, the Teamsters Union under Hoffa is often not run as a bona fide union. As Mr. Hoffa operates it, this is a conspiracy of evil.

Old Nathan Shefferman, who was shrewd enough to pick up some of the biggest corporations in the nation as clients for his labor relations operation and to act as mediator between Beck and Hoffa in the days when Beck still was on top and Hoffa was trying to topple him, thinks Robert Kennedy strengthened Hoffa's position within the Teamsters union. Shefferman wrote a book *The Man in the Middle,* in 1961. In it, he contended that "Jimmy (Hoffa) and young Robert Kennedy were made for each other." He then explained why:

In view of the concept of folklore hero-risen-from-poor-boy, and remembering that Hoffa pitches to his own people without caring much about the general audience, it is easy to understand how the endless jousting with the rich man's son, young Kennedy, brought Hoffa and the Teamsters closer together. Kennedy erred in lending himself to a "get Hoffa" crusade in speeches and writings and interviews, thereby detracting from the judicial nature of the proceedings. At any rate, he aided Jimmy, who became a martyr in the eyes of the Teamsters.

Strangely enough in some very basic ways Jimmy Hoffa and Robert F. Kennedy are men cut from the same pattern. But, by reason of birth, one was cut from roughest burlap and the other from finest silk. It is fascinating to contemplate the routes they would have followed if Hoffa had been born the son of a millionaire in fashionable Brookline, Massachusetts, and Kennedy the son of a poor coal-mine driller in Brazil, Indiana. Both men possess wills of steel. Both live rather simple and basically abstemious lives. Both are devoted husbands and fathers. Both have a national reputation for ruthlessness. Both have envisioned themselves fighting for justice. Neither has permitted seemingly impregnable barriers to halt his rise to the top.

But there is one major and all-important difference between these two men who have staged a clash of Shakespearean proportions for the nation. Kennedy has been guided, even when he has been wrong, by a strong moral consciousness. It is this moral consciousness that makes him the relentless foe of a man he regards as evil—Jimmy Hoffa.

If, as Wellington claimed, the Battle of Waterloo was won on the playing fields at Eton, then it also could be claimed that the New Frontier was launched from the Senate caucus room. The nation first became aware of Jack Kennedy when he lost the 1956 vice-presidential nomination. But it was only an awareness. The nationally televised rackets hearings made Jack Kennedy a national hero. He was not as active in interrogation as a number of other members of the McClellan Committee, but he managed—with his brother coaching behind the scenes—to turn up at opportune moments to ask the right questions, make the right statements and clash with the right witnesses. It even was a help to him in his later primary fights that many television viewers confused the two brothers and somehow regarded Jack as a composite of the tough, dogged counsel and the more aloof and courtly Senator.

The Rackets Committee also was a fertile recruiting field for men who later became stalwarts of the New Frontier—Ken O'Donnell; Pierre Salinger, now the President's press secretary; Carmine Bellino, now a consultant to the President; John Seigenthaler, Robert Kennedy's administrative assistant until he went back to Nashville as editor of the *Tennessean* in the spring of 1962; Ed Guthman, now the Attorney General's press secretary; Wallace Turner, chief information officer for the Department of Health, Education and Welfare until he joined *The New York Times* in 1962; Jim McShane, now U. S. marshal in the District of Columbia; Walter Sheridan, now an assistant to Kennedy at the Justice Department, and, of course, the Attorney General himself.

Not everyone was wildly enthusiastic about Robert Kennedy's performance on the McClellan Committee. But McClellan himself found his chief counsel "dynamic, thorough and unusually competent." He also felt that his judgment and ability as an interrogator improved as the hearings progressed. There were a few

times when McClellan had to overrule him. Other
members of the committee report that McClellan
thought Robert Kennedy showed immaturity at times
and that on one or two occasions he was disturbed by
his treatment of other Senators. But by and large Mc-
Clellan was impressed with Kennedy's work and backed
him to the hilt.

Senator Barry Goldwater approved of Robert Kennedy's conduct of the Rackets Committee except for
his handling of the heralded UAW-Walter Reuther
probe that almost ended the committee. "I don't think
he did as thorough a job of investigation in some areas
as he could have done," says Goldwater. "He was more
interested in the symptoms than in the disease. The
disease is the concentration of power in the hands of
union leaders. All we were seeing was what could happen with that power."

Goldwater also recalls that Robert gave Brother Jack
"a break in interrogating witnesses" but he is not
much disturbed by this.

Senator Karl Mundt contends that in the UAW
probe, Robert Kennedy actually became Reuther's defense attorney, and the prosecution in the case against
the Kohler Company. He also claims that Kennedy
was grossly unfair in his treatment of Senator Carl
Curtis, who was attempting to prove a pattern of violence within Reuther's union. Republican members of
the committee, excepting Senator Ives, always have
charged the Kennedys wanted to halt the investigation
of Reuther because Jack needed the labor chieftain's
support in his presidential bid. It probably is true
that Jack Kennedy sought Reuther's support, but the
record also proves that in the showdown, it was the
Democrats on the committee who forced a public hearing and the calling of Reuther himself.

One Midwestern Republican Senator who served on

the Rackets Committee states in summary: "It was a good television show. The whole thing was run like a good show. Prospective witnesses were screened in advance, and if they didn't seem able to put on a good act, they were never allowed to appear. But it was a show that cost four million dollars of the taxpayers' money, and accomplished very little in reforming union abuses."

Robert Kennedy explains that witnesses had to be screened in advance so their testimony could be verified and their veracity established. In *The Enemy Within*, he says:

> For every witness who was called before the committee we interviewed at least thirty-five. For every hour a witness testified on the stand before the committee, he was interviewed on the average of five hours. For every document that was introduced, five thousand were studied. For every hearing held, there were approximately eight months of intensive investigation, with two investigators from the staff and six accountants from the General Accounting Office.

His own oft-quoted recollection of the pace he set on the McClellan Committee is: "It was like playing Notre Dame every day."

Robert Kennedy left the Committee in 1959 to finish his book, which proved a critical and financial success, and to devote himself full time to his brother's presidential campaign. The committee staff and newspaper reporters who had covered the long investigation gave a big party for him at the National Press Club in October of that year, at the same time that Nikita Khrushchev was visiting in Washington. Within days of that party, the Brothers Kennedy gathered with fourteen advisers, employees, politicians, relatives and friends in Robert's home at Hyannisport, Massachusetts, to exchange views, discuss problems, sift information and to take an organized step forward into the presidential campaign. There had been a spring meeting at Palm Beach and summer meetings in Washington, but at this day-long session strategy was analyzed and perfected and assignments were parceled out. There was, of course, no question about Robert Kennedy's assignment. He was to be manager of his brother's presidential campaign although he was given no specific title.

John Kennedy could travel only one route to Los Angeles if he expected to win the nomination—and that was the long, treacherous road marked "presidential primaries." As a Catholic, a member of the United States Senate and a relatively young man of just forty-two, Jack Kennedy could not expect the old pros who sit in control of convention delegations to see him as a winner or as presidential timber. He had to go to the people. Without the delegate strength and, more importantly, the nationwide publicity to be gained from winning state primaries, Jack Kennedy could not hope for the nomination. Lyndon Johnson was certain to go into convention with an almost solid bloc of Southern votes, plus a scattering of others derived from the men who were his strong allies in the Senate. If Kennedy had to follow the primary route, Johnson had to avoid it. The Texan was assured a huge built-in vote, he had to continue to run the Senate as majority leader, and he could not chance a defeat by John Kennedy in the primaries.

Senator Stuart Symington of Missouri, hopeful but not obsessed with White House ambitions, saw the possibility of a Kennedy-Johnson deadlock and therein his opportunity to emerge as the compromise candidate. But Symington started late, made only a casual attempt to line up votes and placed too much confidence in Harry Truman's claim that primaries are "eyewash." They obviously were "eyewash" in 1952 when Truman manipulated the party machinery in favor of Adlai Stevenson. But Truman seemed not to realize that he lost this power of convention manipulation the day he once more became a private citizen.

Adlai Stevenson, if he actually desired a third ride on the presidential merry-go-round, was willing to wait for the convention to come to him should the Kennedy-Johnson deadlock develop and Symington prove unsuitable.

Only one Democrat felt the need to prove himself in the primaries against Jack Kennedy. And that one was Hubert Humphrey who, for all his eloquence and intellect, was also the weakest candidate of the lot.

The battleground on which Kennedy, the rich, cultured Bostonian, and Humphrey, the voluble Horatio Alger from Minnesota, chose to meet was Wisconsin, that hardy cross-section of Americana where a countryside jeweled with lakes is one of the loveliest in the nation and towns settled in soot are among the ugliest; where political heroes have ranged from Old Bob La Follette to Joe McCarthy; where Catholics dominate the cities and Protestants the farms; where Americans of German, Polish and Scandinavian descent wear their hyphen with ferocious pride.

Before the actual campaign began, Robert Kennedy spent seven days tramping the snow-packed streets of Wisconsin, talking with politicians and voters, determining trouble spots and looking at local Democratic parties.

This tour was important from many aspects, but none so vital as his discovery that the Kennedys had to operate with their own personnel, independent of the state Democratic organization. They were able to recruit to their cause two able men from the Democratic party, State Chairman Patrick J. Lucey and Ivan Nestingen, the Mayor of Madison. But those in command positions—under Robert Kennedy—were Larry O'Brien, Kenneth O'Donnell, Pierre Salinger and others who held membership in that indomitable, hard-working band of stalwarts that the Kennedy brothers had put together.

In the language of the theater, Robert Kennedy was both director and featured player in the dazzling spectacle staged to star his brother in Wisconsin. As manager of the campaign, he directed an amazing network of people, ideas, techniques and actions. As a Kennedy, he appeared at dawn to talk with factory workers when they arrived for their jobs and continued through day and night making speeches on behalf of Jack's candidacy. He was to play this dual role right up to election day, November 8.

Humphrey, who lacked the endless flow of campaign money that the Kennedys had, made the strategic error of relying too much on so-called friends in the state Democratic party and within the upper echelons of organized labor and farm organizations. He had done great favors for them in the Senate and expected reciprocation. When the battle was over, Robert Kennedy said: "That's the mistake that Hubert made. He didn't find out until it was too late that you couldn't depend on the Wisconsin organization."

Jack Kennedy, of course, won the Wisconsin primary. But his victory, 20½ delegates out of 31, was not of the proportions that had been predicted and it failed to halt Humphrey's quest for the presidential nomination. The vote, unfortunately, broke down along religious lines. Kennedy carried the predominantly Catholic districts and Humphrey the heavily Protestant areas. The general conclusion was that

Kennedy could, as expected, win a huge Catholic vote. But what could he do nationwide in a country where Protestants far outnumber Catholics? Wisconsin had not answered that question.

Having defeated Humphrey in Wisconsin, the Kennedys thought the Minnesotan should bow out of the campaign. Instead, Humphrey said he was encouraged by Wisconsin, and aimed for West Virginia, a solidly Protestant and economically depressed state where his record as champion of the working people could be expected to have greater appeal against the wealthy, more moderate Catholic candidate from New England.

Robert Kennedy and Larry O'Brien were weary from the many weeks and long hours of campaigning in Wisconsin. But without a day's rest, they flew to West Virginia the morning after the Wisconsin primary. They were angry. They were determined. They were after Hubert's blood.

In West Virginia, a state where whole counties writhed in financial agony and where Bible Belt distrust of Catholics prevailed, they fashioned a political assault of such overwhelming proportions that Hubert Humphrey, a hapless and hopeless victim, was crushed by it. They saturated the state with volunteer workers, Kennedy campaign literature, telephone calls and television appearances of John Kennedy. Each of West Virginia's eight districts was placed under a Kennedy campaign lieutenant. Jack Kennedy hammered so hard at the religious issue that it became a necessity for a man to vote for him to prove his tolerance. The Kennedys used their influence to reduce Humphrey's money supply. They charged that Humphrey was in the race only as a front man for Johnson and Symington. They scored heavily with public appearances on Kennedy's behalf by Franklin D. Roosevelt, Jr., whose father is deified by the impoverished of West Virginia.

At the end, John Kennedy made a promise that only he could keep (and eventually did). He pledged that if nominated and elected he would take immediate steps to help West Virginia financially. He pointed out that Humphrey could not make such a promise because Humphrey could not possibly win the nomination.

For all their powerful drive, however, the Kennedys were uncertain about West Virginia on the eve of the May 10 election. John Kennedy returned to Washington to await the results in the seclusion of his Georgetown home. *Time* magazine correspondent Hugh Sidey, author of the profile on Robert Kennedy in *The Kennedy Circle,* recalls this incident on the night before the voting began:

> Ethel Kennedy hurried into Charleston to be with Bobby in this dim time. It was raining election eve. Ethel stood at the edge of the airport ramp shielding herself from the mist. Suddenly Hubert Humphrey appeared. His spirits were up, he plainly felt he would win this one. He rushed up to Ethel, gripped her hand. "When this is all in and our temperatures are down some, I hope we can get together with our families," said Hubert. "That was rather sweet of him," said Ethel, staring after him. Then, remembering her own mission of comfort, she rushed off to find the glum Bobby.

Once the vote results began to come in on election night, it did not take the Kennedys long to realize that Jack had scored a decisive victory. About midnight, Robert telephoned Jack in Washington and suggested that he fly out to Charleston. Humphrey already had decided to concede and by 1 a.m. he had dispatched a congratulatory telegram to the Kennedy headquarters in the Kanawha Hotel. Minutes after it arrived, Robert Kennedy walked through wet streets to Humphrey's suite in the Ruffner.

When a proud, brilliant man has just witnessed the collapse of the boldest ambition of his life, there is not much anyone can say. Kennedy understood this. His first words, as he clasped Hubert Humphrey's hand, were: "I just came over to say hello." They were simple, gracious words and Humphrey accepted them as such. The Minnesotan walked back with Robert Kennedy through those same wet streets to the Kanawha Hotel, and there announced that "I am no longer a candidate for the Democratic presidential nomination." There were tears in almost everyone's eyes, including those of Robert Kennedy.

By winning sixty-five per cent of the vote in West Virginia, where Catholics make up less than four per cent of the populace, Jack Kennedy moved within grasp of the big prize. He and his brother knew this. But they had to keep up the momentum they had gained. Long ago they had learned a bit of sage advice from their father: "Never take anything for granted."

Jack Kennedy campaigned against the entire presidential field—Johnson, Symington, Humphrey and favorite son Wayne Morse in Oregon—and won. Oregon was the last of the primaries. But he had behind him victories in New Hampshire, Wisconsin, West Virginia, Nebraska, Maryland and Indiana—and no defeats. In addition, the Kennedys had forced or negotiated lucrative delegate deals in Ohio, California, New York, Illinois, Michigan and other big states. They had broken the Solid South by picking up delegates in such Johnson-territory states as North Carolina and Alabama.

Robert Kennedy arrived in Los Angeles six weeks before the Democratic national convention was called to order in the Sports Arena. Working in the Biltmore Hotel, he put to superb use one of the major lessons he had learned from the 1956 vice-presidential fight. The makeshift Kennedy communications system between delegates and the Kennedy persuaders had broken down badly in 1956. At Los Angeles this error was not repeated. Robert Kennedy utilized walkie-talkies and telephones to keep up-to-the-minute contact among his eighth-floor command post in the Biltmore, a cottage on the Arena grounds, and the convention floor.

One of the most dramatic moments of the convention occurred when Adlai Stevenson walked into the Arena to sit with the Illinois delegation. The popular twice-defeated presidential nominee instantly became the eye of a wild hurricane of sentiment, curiosity and renewed hopes. For a full twenty minutes, the Arena was in pandemonium as police fought to get Stevenson safely off the floor. It seemed obvious that the galleries were packed with Stevensonites. Within an hour after the Stevenson demonstration Robert Kennedy and his chief lieutenants were on the convention floor, making certain that the forty men they had watching over the individual state delegations were keeping their delegations in check.

When the hour for the balloting arrived, Jack Kennedy was sitting in a rented apartment on North Rossmore in Beverly Hills. Robert was in the cottage just outside the Sports Arena.

Angela Novello recalls that during the afternoon Bob relaxed in the cottage and showed no great strain of pressure. He was certain in his own mind that his brother had a first-ballot victory sewed up. When the nominating speeches ended, he said to Angie: "They're going to start balloting. You should go in." He handed her a ticket and she entered the Arena.

Jack telephoned about this same time to determine whether his calculation of the votes they expected was the same as his brother's. They were within one-half vote of each other. Bob watched the tally build up until Wyoming put Jack Kennedy over the magic 761 votes needed for nomination. The count went almost exactly as the Kennedys had expected.

As he did with every important move in the campaign, Jack Kennedy consulted his brother on the choice of Lyndon Johnson as the vice-presidential nominee and Bob agreed the choice was wise.

When the convention was over, Jack flew to Hyannisport to rest. But Robert Kennedy was at work within a few days in the offices he had rented in a Washington office building at the foot of Capitol Hill. He also took over an office in the Democratic national committee. To those who suggested he take a brief rest, he snapped: "We can rest in November."

Robert Kennedy continued in constant motion in Washington while the Republicans in Chicago were nominating Richard Nixon and Henry Cabot Lodge to run against the Kennedy-Johnson ticket. He was appalled at the inefficiency he found at Democratic national headquarters. But rather than attempt to fire and hire with the campaign under way he used the people already in employ and put his own top assistants in charge of them. At the convention Senator Henry Jackson of Washington had been named National Chairman, and Robert was appointed Official Campaign Manager. Byron White was brought in to run the volunteers for Kennedy and Congressman Frank Thompson of New Jersey was placed in command of a nationwide registration drive. But Robert Kennedy was the motivating force in the whole operation.

He instinctively understood the moves he should make and that his brother would expect him to make.

Byron White recalls: "Bob always was happiest when he had to make eighteen to twenty speeches a day. He wanted to get going early in the morning. He hated to sit around half of the day. He had a very sharp idea of what was the effective and the not effective thing to do."

One of his most magnificently brutal performances was staged in New York where the Democratic party was split down the middle between Tammany and a reform element led by Mrs. Eleanor Roosevelt, former Senator Herbert Lehman and former Air Force Secretary Thomas Finletter.

Two weeks after the Democratic convention, Robert Kennedy and Byron White flew to New York to, as White says, "try to make some sense out of that organization up here." "At a meeting with the reform group, Bob made it plain that he was interested in electing his brother," says White. "He was straightforward. He made it pretty clear there were some things you could put up with and some things you couldn't."

Time magazine quoted him as telling the reformers: "Gentlemen, I don't give a damn if the state and county organizations survive after November, and I don't give a damn if you survive. I want to elect John F. Kennedy." His listeners did not like such rough talk but they agreed to do what he demanded—to work together for the election of Jack Kennedy.

But, as in the Wisconsin primary, Robert Kennedy did not put his brother's campaign in the hands of those already entrenched in the party. He placed a Kennedy co-ordinator in charge of each of thirty important states. These generally were men brought in from outside the state so that they would be above the local disputes. "Every state had some kind of a factional fight," explains Kennedy. "If you have a man there who can settle it, it is invaluable."

Of all the issues John Kennedy faced in the 1960

presidential campaign, none was as deep-seated in the consciousness of the electorate or as fraught with political peril as the question of his Catholicism.

At the beginning of his quest for the Democratic presidential nomination, when he was just a handsome, intelligent and little-known Senator from the nation's ninth most populous state, John Kennedy's religion was an asset. It set him apart from all other serious aspirants and gave him an individuality that he otherwise would not have possessed. It also gave him an initial groundswell of support among Catholics who wanted to see one of their own in the White House and among non-Catholics who wanted to see an end to religious prejudice in presidential balloting.

The bias that bars a man from public office because of his religious affiliation has, of course, been a cancer within the national political anatomy since the earliest days of the Republic. But it is a disease on which many office holders thrive. Some stimulate its growth. Some acquiesce to it. Some are its unwilling victims. In every section of the country there are states or counties or cities or congressional districts where a man must be of a particular faith to win election to office. In one area, he must be a Protestant. In another, he must be a Catholic. In a third, he must be a Jew.

Jack Kennedy's Catholicism had been an assist when he ran against Henry Cabot Lodge in Massachusetts in 1952. It had been both a help and a drawback when he met Hubert Humphrey on the frozen Wisconsin prairie in the early spring of 1960. It had started as the worst of liabilities and then was turned into at least a minor asset in West Virginia.

If religion is to affect a man's political career, he must decide whether he is to let it hurt him or make it help him. In West Virginia, the Kennedys determined that they could not let the candidate's Catholicism defeat them. They had to use it as an instrument of advancement rather than rejection. The issue was forced on them. They in turn fired it back at the forcers, and Hubert Humphrey was laid to rest—the innocent victim of his friends and his foe.

Jack Kennedy was not Alfred E. Smith in personality, speech or background. He also was not going to be Al Smith on the crucial religious issue.

After his overwhelming defeat by Herbert Hoover in 1928, Al Smith cried out an angry charge against the nation. "The most un-American and undemocratic issue that could be raised against any man was raised against me—and that was the question of my religion."

For thirty-two years Smith's accusation hung suspended over the American people without being refuted or substantiated. Smith obviously was hurt badly by his membership in the Catholic Church. But who can say that he was not hurt equally by his brown derby, his sidewalks-of-New York speech, his advocation of repeal in an era when the people were reveling in a very wet prohibition, and Republican prosperity. In 1960 history restated the challenge, minus the derby, the Eastside accent, or the issue of repeal. Only Republican prosperity was back for a try at winning votes, and it was hardly persuasive among the jobless of Pennsylvania, Kentucky, West Virginia and other states.

Jack Kennedy forcefully stated the case against religious bias on September 13, 1960, when he appeared before the Greater Houston Ministerial Association in Texas. The future president reasserted his belief in separation of church and state, and stated that he was under no obligation to the Vatican in secular matters. One month later, an incident occurred in Indiana that involved Robert Kennedy in his dual role of campaign manager and brother of the presidential nominee and indicated something of the attitude the Kennedy's had adopted toward the religious problem.

At 2 o'clock one autumn morning, Robert Kennedy flew into Dress Memorial Airport prepared to make fourteen speeches in Southern Indiana. He was met at the airport by Clinton Green, a veteran behind-the-scenes political operator whose service in the Democratic party ran back to the days of Indiana's most glamorous vote-seeker, Paul V. McNutt.

Green did not wait around the airport until 2 a.m. just to act as official greeter. He had a far more important mission to take up with Robert Kennedy before he set off through the Hoosier hills where the Ku Klux Klan once had been a tremendous power. Matthew Welsh, a slender, patrician State Senator, was running for governor on the Democratic ticket and feared that the Catholic issue could defeat him. Welsh himself is a member of the Christian Church. But his wife and their twin daughters are Catholics, and this affiliation was kept in the background of Welsh's campaign. Green had been sent by the Welshmen to implore Robert Kennedy not to bring up the religious issue in Indiana.

"I knew the only chance I would have to talk to Bob Kennedy was riding in the car from the airport to the hotel," said Green later. "So on the ride to the hotel, I told him what I had been sent to say."

Green was standing outside Indiana's big limestone Statehouse as he recalled the incident. "I might just as well have been talking to that wall over there. He listened and he didn't say anything. But, you know what he said [in his speeches]."

As Robert Kennedy rolled through the autumn-hued hills of Southern Indiana that day, he criticized the speed of his motorcade and the use of a police escort with siren and, in the words of one local Democrat, demonstrated "a tendency to be a prima donna." He also ignored the request of his hosts that he steer clear of the Catholic issue.

Oscar Handlin, Al Smith's biographer, cited Indiana as one of the two states in the nation in which the Ku Klux Klan had been especially influential during the 1920s. The other state was Oregon. By 1960 the KKK was long gone from power but the strong ferment of religious prejudice still bubbled beneath the political surface in the heavily Protestant Hoosier state.

Robert Kennedy, whose single aim was to elect his brother president, apparently decided there was no better place to preach his lesson of religious tolerance than in the land where the Klan but three decades before was a political power.

He first pointed out to his audiences that one of the "burdens" his brother had brought with him to leadership of the Democratic party was his Catholicism. Bob said this certainly had been a factor in Al Smith's defeat and added that although it still was a "problem" in Indiana, the state Democratic party was supporting John Kennedy.

Recalling the West Virginia primary, he said: "I went in one county and the chairman said to me, 'It was nice of you to come visit us. It was very nice to see you. We got two Catholics and four Negroes in this town.' In many counties they never had seen a Catholic before. They thought a Catholic was somebody who walked around with horns on his head. They were convinced the Senator [Kennedy] had the Pope in the back of his car and was going to let him out if he ever got a chance."

Kennedy continued his assault on religious prejudice in a more serious vein. He said: "It seems to me that Senator Kennedy has proved over and over that he is a loyal American citizen, as my older brother proved it by giving his life for his country. In 1943, Senator Kennedy was in the South Pacific and was badly wounded in the service of his country. . . .

"It seems to me we have to look at his record and at the record of Catholics here in the United States. They have performed major services for their country. I cannot believe we are going to say to thirty-five or forty million Catholics in the United States that after two hundred years, that a Catholic is not liable and is not able to be President of the United States because he might be disloyal. . . .

"We can say we expect Mr. Adenauer to be a bastion against communism in Germany, that we think he is a wonderful patriot, that he is a wonderful man in standing up to the Soviet Union, that we expect the same thing from Mr. de Gaulle, that we expect the same thing from some of these other leaders in Europe. Many of these leaders are Catholic as are Mr. Adenauer and Mr. de Gaulle. Can we say that if they were born here in the United States they wouldn't be liable to be President?"

When the ordeal of that day was over, Green said: "I realized that the Kennedy people had come to a conclusion, and were taking a calculated risk. They were going to talk about religion. They were the ones who brought up the religious issue and kept it alive. It wasn't the Republicans."

The sentiments spoken by Democrat Green were echoed by Republicans in Richard Nixon's headquarters.

But Ken O'Donnell explains: "The Kennedys didn't want to discuss the religious issue at first. But after [Dr. Norman Vincent] Peale and [Dr. Daniel] Poling and the fake Knights of Columbus oath, they had no choice. I personally don't think we gained by bringing it up. You don't get anybody to vote on a fair play appeal."

O'Donnell adds: "If Kennedy had been a Protestant, he would have buried Nixon."

Through the long months of the campaign, Robert Kennedy always was available in person or by telephone to his fellow workers. He also possessed the unique faculty of being able to decide important problems on the spot. "He's got a direct line to the candidate," said Ken O'Donnell during the campaign. "When you go to Bobby it's like going to the chief. He speaks for the candidate. You always get action."

Jack Kennedy, near the end of the campaign, best summed up the immeasurable value of his brother's talents and advice in these words: "I don't even have to think about organization. I just show up. Bobby's easily the best man I've ever seen. He's the hardest worker. He's the greatest organizer. . . . I'll take his word over anybody's."

At strategic moments late in the battle, Robert Kennedy shifted funds and workers from states that appeared hopeless—like Oklahoma—to those—like Illinois—that seemed to need a little extra cash and activity to go for Jack Kennedy. He kept controversial figures like Frank Sinatra and Walter Reuther off the Kennedy campaign trail. He added millions of Democratic voters to the registration rolls. He avoided the perilous pitfalls that Adlai Stevenson had fallen into time and again in 1956.

When the votes finally were counted from the biggest election day turnout in American history, Jack Kennedy had defeated Richard Nixon by 112,881 votes out of 68,832,818. In a vote so close, the organization and registration drive operated under the astute and despotic leadership of the younger Kennedy may have decided the outcome. Certainly no campaign manager in history worked harder, longer and more selflessly than did Robert Kennedy to elect his brother as 35th President of the United States.

Looking back over the accomplishments of his career, Robert Kennedy says: "I was pleased we won in 1952. That campaign was very tough. The work on the McClellan Committee also was very tough and gratifying. Writing my book also was gratifying. But the most important of all was the presidential campaign of 1960."

Chapter Ten
Beyond the New Frontier

ONE OF ROBERT KENNEDY'S PRIZED POSSESSIONS IN A home filled with valuable mementos of Kennedy family life and the American past is a cigarette box presented to him after his brother had won the Democratic presidential nomination in 1960.

The box is without adornment, except for this message inscribed across its top:

ROBERT F. KENNEDY
When I'm Through, How About You?
Democratic National Convention
Los Angeles, 1960

Scrawled almost illegibly beneath the inscription is the signature of the donor—John F. Kennedy.

Jack Kennedy, who shuns the sentimental, presented the gift to his brother as a lighthearted token of gratitude for the monumental job he performed on the long, harrowing road to the convention and during the ordeal of Los Angeles itself. The Kennedys say the inscription, which seemingly points the way to a family dynasty in the Presidency, was written in jest. This may be. It is not improbable, however, that the future could prove this jest one of the most prophetic in American political history.

President Kennedy says he honestly does not know what course Robert will follow when his days on the New Frontier have ended.

"I've thought about that myself," said the President as he began his second year in office. "But I don't know. I haven't talked to him about it."

Should the Chief Executive discuss this matter with his brother, he probably would not find himself greatly enlightened. For Robert Kennedy is a man wholly preoccupied with the present and unconcerned about his own future. He is so deeply involved in his responsibilities as a member of the Cabinet and confidant to the President that he has not attempted to chart his career beyond its current point.

"As far as I'm concerned," says Robert Kennedy, "I have no future beyond this job. I am here—now—thinking about this work and not about what I am going to be doing in the future."

He concedes that many skeptics will not accept such a statement. They will not believe that as aggressive and ambitious a young man as Robert Kennedy is not possessed of a secret grand design to project himself onward and upward.

"But this is the way I've always acted," the Attorney General explains. "When I was on the McClellan Committee I didn't plan my next step and when I was on the presidential campaign I didn't plan my next step. Everything's always worked out reasonably well without planning."

Robert Kennedy is willing to make only one positive statement about his future.

"I'm certainly not going to stay on as Attorney General for eight years," he says.

Then, with a sly grin, he adds: "Perhaps I should think about what I'm going to do. I'll be less than forty when this is over. Maybe I'll retire."

Does Robert Kennedy aspire to the Presidency? "It's not an ambition of mine," he states succinctly. But he expects to remain vitally interested in politics and does not discount the possibility that events and circumstances could so arrange themselves in the far future that he might become interested in obtaining the highest office in the land. He also concedes that one day he would like to seek election to public office, but the question is: What office, when and where?

The prospect of his running for office is one that excites his wife, Ethel. Not only does she admit that she wants her energetic young husband to be elected on his own, she even has had one elective job picked out for him.

"The Massachusetts governorship needs him," says Ethel. "It's a mess." She adds her confidence that the governorship also is an office that Bob would like to occupy.

The complicating factor in this proposal, as both the President and the Attorney General point out, is the political ambition of their younger brother, Teddy. After Jack Kennedy was elected President, Teddy returned to Massachusetts to launch his own political career and is running this year for the Senate seat once occupied by the President. His Republican opponent, if both can win their respective party nominatons, will be George Cabot Lodge, son of the President's old political foe of both the 1952 Senate race and the 1960 presidential fight, Henry Cabot Lodge.

Should Teddy emerge the victor, he would have only two years left to serve of Jack Kennedy's old six-year term. He therefore would have to seek re-election in 1964 in the same election and on the same state ballot with President Kennedy. To add Robert's name to that ballot as candidate for Governor would be an oversaturation of Kennedys—even for Massachusetts.

If Robert Kennedy were to return to Massachusetts to seek election, he could not do so before 1966 at the earliest. But President Kennedy says he will not do this. The President believes that Teddy's plunge into Bay State politics has ended, at least for some time, any chance of the other brother making the same plunge.

Because of the civil rights issue, his Catholic religion, his Yankee birth and the seeming indestructibility of the conservative political machine of Senator Harry Flood Byrd, Robert Kennedy presumably would be doomed to failure if he attempted a statewide race in Virginia, the state in which he now lives.

There was talk a few years ago that he would attempt to establish a voting residence in Ethel's home state of Connecticut and seek office there, but he has made no attempt to do so. One close friend of the Kennedys says he had hoped Bob would give up his home at Hickory Hill and move instead into one of the Maryland suburbs of the District of Columbia. In this way, he could seek the governorship of Maryland, a state that has many facets in common with Massachusetts. But, again, Bob has shown no inclination to make such a move. He continues to live at Hickory Hill and vote at Hyannisport, Massachusetts.

But John Kennedy says he expects Robert Kennedy

"to be with me"—to be a part of the New Frontier—as long as he is President. There is no doubt that as long as the President feels the need to have his brother in his Administration, he will remain. He also will undertake any task assigned him by the President.

During the summer of 1961, in the wake of the ill-fated attempt of anti-Castro Cubans to invade their homeland, there was speculation in Washington that the President would make Robert Kennedy director of the Central Intelligence Agency to replace the retiring chief, Allen W. Dulles. But instead the President summoned John A. McCone, former Chairman of the Atomic Energy Commission, back to Washington for the Dulles job.

There may be no other post in John Kennedy's Administration that would provide Robert Kennedy with the base he has at Justice to branch out in all directions—both domestic and international—that interest him and assist the President.

He was asked recently if he had any regrets over taking the Attorney Generalship rather than a high post in the Department of State or the Pentagon. He replied: "I'm pleased where I am now. There are a great many areas where a lot of things can be done. And I also am able to be involved to some extent in foreign policy and national defense."

If Robert Kennedy does not plan to serve a full eight years as Attorney General and is barred by his brothers' political activities from seeking election in Massachusetts, what does he plan to do? President Kennedy partially answers this by stating that he expects him to serve in his Administration unto the end and by adding that "it is quite possible" he will shift his brother to some other top job in government.

Robert Kennedy's future is beginning to stir speculation in the nation's capital, where the presidential guessing game is not just played quadrennially but is a favorite parlor pastime on almost any night of any year.

Columnist Doris Fleeson suggested in November 1961 that a political royal family was a-borning in the United States. She said Teddy's plan to run for the Senate in Massachusetts "has had the rather odd effect of turning the old talk about the dynastic potential of the Kennedys from jest to earnest conversation."

Miss Fleeson added: "Suddenly the politicians are asking whether 1968 will see another Kennedy—the Attorney General—running against Lyndon Johnson for the Democratic nomination for President. The thought of starting to choose up sides on that one is a rather chilling one in some places—including Texas."

If John Kennedy serves two full terms as President, he will leave the White House on January 20, 1969. At that time Robert will be forty-three, the same age as Jack when he became President.

As President and head of his political party, John Kennedy will have the power to determine who the Democrats nominate as his successor. President Harry S. Truman used this authority ultimately in 1952 to seal the nomination of Adlai E. Stevenson and President Theodore Roosevelt in 1908 dictated the nomination of William Howard Taft.

It is not probable, however, that a President-politician of John Kennedy's subtlety and skill would attempt so blatant a move as to decree that the Democratic party nominate his brother. If the relationship between the White House and the Vice President is as cordial and co-operative in 1968 as in 1962, Lyndon Johnson, who then will be sixty years old, should be the obvious front runner for the Democratic presidential nomination. The proud, astute Texan must have had this in mind when he agreed in Los Angeles in

1960 to be John Kennedy's running mate. It was all too apparent at the Democratic conclave of that year that even as able a senator as Johnson from a state like Texas, with its particular interests of oil and gas and its problems of civil rights, could not be nominated by a party which depends so heavily upon the support of religious and racial minorities, organized labor, liberal intellectuals, and big-city dwellers of the North.

As Vice President, however, Johnson has been able to divorce himself from the purely regional issues that have stood between him and the Democratic presidential nomination. He has begun to construct an impressive record as the Administration's chief spokesman in the fight against job discrimination for reasons of race and as trouble-shooter and ambassador of goodwill to the areas of the world that are in turmoil.

What is even more important to any presidential hopes that might be harbored by either Johnson or Robert Kennedy is the fact that the nation has been moving slowly into a new era of White House politics. For decade upon decade, from the Reconstruction Era to the Nuclear Age, the man most strategically situated to seek and win a presidential nomination was the governor of a big state—and especially the Governor of New York. But now governors who have risen to power strictly through state politics and lack any background in international affairs no longer are the dominant contenders in the presidential fight. Since the great problems facing America are international, the people and their political parties seem to demand a candidate of broad experience and schooling in world affairs—an adroit and much-traveled Vice President like Richard M. Nixon (or Lyndon Johnson); a distinguished soldier-statesman like Dwight D. Eisenhower; a senator like John Kennedy who has specialized in foreign affairs; or possibly a Cabinet officer (like Robert Kennedy) who has participated in formulation of national policy.

Even the two governors who have been most actively involved in presidential politics in recent years—the Democrats' twice-nominated Adlai Stevenson and a Republican hopeful, Nelson Rockefeller—had served in the Federal Government, and especially the Department of State, before becoming involved in state elections.

No one can predict the political situation within the Democratic party when 1968 rolls around. If John Kennedy is defeated in 1964, he probably will be ready for another try. If he is re-elected, a number of contenders for his job will have appeared on the horizon—in the Cabinet, in Congress, in the state capitals. Stevenson, always possessed of a militant and devoted following, presumably will be too old at sixty-eight to seek a third nomination. Senator Hubert Humphrey of Minnesota, a brilliant man with a thorough comprehension of an amazing range of issues, will be fifty-seven at the time and possibly ready for a second crack at the Presidency.

By experience and knowledge of issues, Robert Kennedy should be a logical contender for the Democratic presidential nomination after eight years of service in the retiring Administration. He will have sat in the highest councils, helped formulate the most critical policies, presided over a great department, and conferred with the world's leaders. His brother already has demolished the age and religious barriers. Three Republicans—Taft, Hoover and Eisenhower—have proved that a man of stature can be elected president without having previously run for public office. Excepting the competition he might face from Johnson and other contenders, Robert Kennedy's biggest hurdle would be the question of political dynasty arising from his relationship to the President.

George Washington abruptly ended any thought of an American monarchy in 1782 when he severely rebuked Colonel Lewis Nicola for suggesting that he become King. But beginning with Washington's own Vice President, John Adams, the family has been a successful and attractive force in the nation's elections.

Succeeding generations of Adamses and Lodges in Massachusetts, Roosevelts in New York, Tafts in Ohio, Stevensons in Illinois, La Follettes in Wisconsin, Longs in Louisiana, Byrds in Virginia, and countless others in various states, have triumphed in the political arena, in part or in whole, because they bore names associated with popular leaders of the past.

It was an asset to John Quincy Adams that he was the son of the second President; to Benjamin Harrison that he was the grandson of the ninth President, and to Franklin D. Roosevelt that he was the cousin of the twenty-sixth President. In none of these instances, however, was there any basis for charging a family with attempting to create a dynasty in the Presidency. A twenty-eight-year period separated the election of John Adams from the election of John Quincy Adams, and a forty-eight-year period the election of William Henry Harrison from the election of Benjamin Harrison. Teddy Roosevelt succeeded to the Presidency on the death of William McKinley in 1901 and it was not until thirty-one years later that Franklin Roosevelt was elected President and by the opposition party.

Never has there been an attempt by a President's brother, son, grandson or other relative to become that President's immediate successor in the White House. But never has any President so prepared a relative for White House occupancy as has John Kennedy by making his brother a dynamic participant in the major activities and decisions of his administration.

If Robert Kennedy has national political aspirations, but feels for certain reasons—the President's commitment to Johnson and the dynasty controversy —that it would be unwise to seek the presidential nomination in 1968, he could run for Vice President on a ticket headed by Johnson. There were serious proposals in 1960 that Richard Nixon choose Milton Eisenhower for his running mate and they did not stir up much criticism.

When Paul Butler, who was Democratic national chairman at the time Jack Kennedy was nominated and was accused of using his high party position to aid Kennedy, was interviewed prior to his death, he refused to express any specific opinion about the President or his brother. But Butler did say: "I see no reason why a brother to the President could not be elected President, if you offered an attractive enough combination of brothers."

Senator Barry Goldwater of Arizona, himself a Republican presidential hopeful—but also a friend and admirer of Robert Kennedy's—says: "Depending on how Jack Kennedy's administration fares, I think Bob could run for the Senate from Massachusetts. But outside of that I think he is as far as he's going unless his brother puts him on the Supreme Court."

"As of now, I don't think he can be elected President," says Goldwater. Then, with a wry smile, he adds: "But, hell, I said that of Jack too!"

One friend of both Kennedys, a New York advertising executive who did yeoman service in the 1960 presidential race, says "Bobby for President? I hadn't thought about that, but it's something I could get excited about. I'd love to work for Bobby for President."

Kenneth O'Donnell, who probably has worked more closely with the two brothers over the years than any other person, shies away from talk of Robert Kennedy for President. But he maintains the primary difference between Bob and Jack is one of maturity and experience. It is his opinion that in his reactions, his interests and his approach to government, Bob basically is Jack, minus eight years of additional growth.

One of Washington's most astute journalists, a man who has watched both Kennedys at close range since 1956, believes Robert Kennedy would make a better president than Jack. Comparing Jack's handling of Cuba with Bob's handling of the Alabama Freedom Riders' riot, he is convinced that the Attorney General demonstrated the greater faculty for command decision.

Goldwater and Senator Karl Mundt, Robert Kennedy's old nemesis from McCarthy-McClellan Committee days, have discussed this question of which brother would make the better president and have found themselves in sharp disagreement on it.

These are Goldwater's views: "It's not difficult to compare the two brothers. I think Bob is by far a better organizer. I think he sees and understands things more quickly than does the President.

"The President has a better background position to work from. He has trained himself in a number of fields. But, with Bob, decisions would be more quickly reached and would come from a fewer number of minds. If the decisions were only those of the two men, I don't think their decisions would differ greatly. But Bob would have fewer people to clutter up his thinking. Not only would decisions be more quickly reached, but I think they would be better decisions."

Mundt contends that Robert Kennedy "has no political future on the national political scene because he has no personality to sell for president or vice president."

The North Dakotan adds: "Barry and I have discussed this and we disagree on it. But I'd much rather live in a country with Jack Kennedy as President than with Bobby. I've got much more confidence in Jack Kennedy to meet problems of strength and size than in Bobby. Jack has a broadness and a bigness. He recognizes there are other people with noble purposes and convictions. Bobby develops anathema and hatefulness toward those who disagree with him. He's a guy of blacks and whites. He has this in quantity size bottles. Jack has it in pint size bottles. Jack has a much greater personality."

It is, of course, impossible to know what the White House will do to the character and personality of a man once he becomes President. The most quoted political misjudgment of modern time was Walter Lippmann's 1933 description of Franklin D. Roosevelt as an amiable man who lacked strong conviction or a firm grasp of public affairs. There was little in Harry Truman's political background or his Senate service to indicate that he possessed the courage and the wisdom to initiate the Truman doctrine, Greek-Turkish aid, the Marshall Plan, the defense of South Korea, and American participation in the North Atlantic Treaty Organization. Too much was expected of Dwight D. Eisenhower and he disappointed admirers who had expected him to exert the powers of the Presidency with bolder authority.

There is about Robert Kennedy an infectious and unaffected warmth that endears him to his associates. This trait, combined with an inclination to speak bluntly when irritated, gives him something of a Trumanesque quality. But in his love of the rugged life, his craving for action, and his bullmoose courage

against all enemies, as in his small, muscular physique
and his rather high-pitched voice, Robert Kennedy also
is a latter-day Teddy Roosevelt.

He is a spunky, intelligent young man who still may
lack the finesse and vast political awareness of his
brother. But he has proved in every job he has undertaken that he will turn every resource of energy and
talent to the task until he has conquered it. He is better suited by temperament and inclination to serve in
an executive or administrative post than in a legislative body, where talk too often is long and action is
short.

Robert Kennedy campaigned extensively and ex-
haustively for his brother in 1960 and learned what is
required of a presidential nominee. He also has grown
in his understanding of peoples and governments since
assuming the demanding role of number-two man on
the New Frontier. His record on such issues as civil
rights, trust-busting, organized crime, communist sub-
version, the extremists of the far right, and friendship
for the newly emerging nations is one that most Democrats would find palatable.

But Robert Kennedy never has had to campaign for
himself. He has not had to face an erudite presidential
opponent in televised debate. He has not hour after
hour, day after day for months on end been forced to
hide his explosive nature behind a façade of smiles
and charm. He may or may not have faced up to the
fact that his terrier-like personality and slight physical
stature do not create the same presidential image as the
cool intellectualism and towering poise of his older
brother.

Yet Robert Kennedy never has been deterred by the
old dogmas of politics. He and Jack already have
slain too many sacred cows to be frightened by the ones
that still roam the political fields. Should Bob one day

decide to go after the Presidency, he would do so with the support of a vast organization of family and friends, the financial assistance of a huge war chest, and all the ferocity and determination he poured into Jack Kennedy's campaign.

To the Presidency, as to any other office he might attain, Robert Kennedy would bring an inquisitive and probing mind and a passion for action and hard work. He would make loyal friends and bitter enemies. He probably would steer a course of moderate liberalism, one that would continue America's advance into the future without veering far left of center.

Many a self-styled pundit on the Washington scene claims Robert Kennedy could not possibly win the Presidency as his brother's successor because the American people are unequivocally opposed to establishment of a family dynasty in the White House. Among these individuals and their predecessors in dissemination of false political calculations are the ones who said Jack Kennedy could not win the Democratic presidential nomination or the election in 1960 because of his religion and his youth and that Franklin D. Roosevelt could not be re-elected in 1940 because the American people were dead set against a third term.

The American people will set aside their traditions and even their prejudices for a political figure who has captured their fancy. It is safe to bet that a majority of them would willingly have expunged the 22nd Amendment from the Constitution in 1960 to permit Dwight Eisenhower a third term. Should the people in 1968 or in a succeeding election find themselves still in need of Kennedy leadership, they might decide to forget their fears of dynasty and stake their hopes on Robert Francis Kennedy.

① Sidey, Hugh. The Kennedy Circle

② Kennedy, Robert. The Enemy Within.